THIS SIDE OF THE

GL🌐BAL WALL

WALL

GARY MILLER

ISBN: 978-1-941213-76-6

Image credits: All images copyrighted by Shutterstock except the following:

page 7 and 199: Illustration by Nathan Wright

page 15: top right, Istockphoto

page 20 and 190: stone wall grapic, Graphicstock

page 30 and 126: CAM photobank

page 81: Istockphoto

page 150: Illustration by Jerron Hess

Printed in India

Second printing: February 2016

Published by:
TGS International
P.O. Box 355, Berlin, Ohio 44610 USA
Phone: 330-893-4828 | Fax: 330-893-2305 | www.tgsinternational.com

TGS001185

Contents

[4]

Introduction—
THE WALL

The city of Samaria was under siege. It had been surrounded by the Syrian army, and the inhabitants were slowly starving. The Bible tells us that during this time several men decided to go to the Syrians and plead for mercy. These men were lepers—the outcasts of Samaria. They realized that death from starvation was imminent and they had little to lose. So one night they headed toward the Syrian army's camp. As the men cautiously approached the outermost tents, their minds must have raced with possible entreaties. No doubt they fully expected to be annihilated by the enemy, and the most they could hope for was a quick and merciful death.

We can only imagine their shock when they discovered that the invaders had fled in haste, leaving all their belongings, food, and wealth behind. Imagine the sight! Starving men suddenly surrounded by an abundance of food and wealth. How they must have attacked that food! The Bible says they satisfied their immediate hunger and then began hurriedly carrying their newfound treasures to places of hiding.

But in the middle of running back and forth, they must have stopped and looked at each other in disbelief. "Why, it was just yesterday that we were starving! Just yesterday we were longing for a crust of bread, and now we have more food than we can store. Just a short time ago we were preparing to die, and now we have more wealth than we can carry."

And then they saw the wall.

Right beside them was the city wall. In the middle of their festive merriment, they had forgotten that just over that wall, others were still starving. They had forgotten the dying children, the emaciated bodies, and the ravaging hunger. They had forgotten the discouragement, the misery, and the pain. They had forgotten the other side of the wall.

When they finally came to their senses, they said to each other, "Something is not right here. We are suffering from overeating, have more things than we can use, and are already struggling with storage dilemmas. And just over that wall, people are starving!"[1]

Our world today has many similarities to this Biblical account. A few of us have too much. We struggle with obesity, have difficulty getting closet doors shut, and have more Bibles around the house than time to read them. Meanwhile, on the other side of the wall, masses of people lack clothing, nutritious food, and a Christian witness. Some children are told to clean up their plates, while others have never seen a full one. It is a world of astonishing imbalance.

If you live in the United States of America, you are living in an amazing time and place. In fact, it is so unusual that it is hard to develop accurate viewpoints and a proper perception of our world. America[a] has experienced peace and prosperity for so long that its citizens have come to view affluence as normal, and plenty as a universal right. Even those regarded as poor in the United States have what they need. Never has there been a country or a time in history so prosperous, and it epitomizes the wealthy side of the global wall.

Sometimes it's good to back up and get a clearer picture of global reality. To do this, we will look at four basic areas:

---

[a] In this book, America always refers to the United States of America.

1. The Global Wealth Wall

The huge disparity in wealth separating developed countries from developing ones.

2. If America Were a Village

What if America were shrunk to a small village of 100 people? What would that village look like?

3. The Uniqueness of Our Time

A look at history and some rapid changes that make our setting unique, providing unprecedented opportunity.

4. A Question You Need to Answer

The Global Wealth

WALL

The Great Global Inequality

Let's begin by looking at the great global inequality in our world. Imagine for a moment there has just been a giant garage sale. All the land, the buildings, the machinery, the vehicles on the road—everything of value on the earth has been sold, and now the proceeds are piled up on the table. All the income from the large corporations and small businesses, everything down to the small dish of coins on your bedroom dresser, is on the table in front of you.

How much would all this be worth? In other words, what is the total wealth on the globe right now?

TOTAL WEALTH =

$241

Trillion

POOR   RICH
♦♦♦

Economists estimate that all the wealth on the globe would add up to $241 trillion. That is a huge, mind-boggling number! But how is this great amount of wealth distributed among the people on our planet?[2]

Imagine shrinking the world's population to 100 people, with each of the small figures across the bottom representing 70 million people. Now picture the poorest on the left and the wealthiest on the right. Obviously the rich have more and the poor less, but how do you think this $241 trillion is distributed, and how great is the disparity?

TOTAL WEALTH = $241 TRILLION

3%
OF THE
WORLD'S WEALTH

97%
OF THE
WORLD'S WEALTH

POOR

RICH

It is estimated that the poorest 69 people control only 3% of the world's wealth. These are the people who struggle to provide the basic necessities of food and clothing for their families. Things like education and good medical care are completely out of reach for the majority of this group.[3]

But while 69 of these people are struggling to survive, the other 31 are enjoying the remaining 97% of the wealth. What a tremendous disparity! And while much of that wealth is in the hands of a few extremely wealthy people farthest to the right, all of those living in the rich portion are living lives beyond the wildest dreams of the global poor.

But let's try to visualize this great disparity another way.

THE GLOBAL WEALTH WALL

3% of the World's Wealth

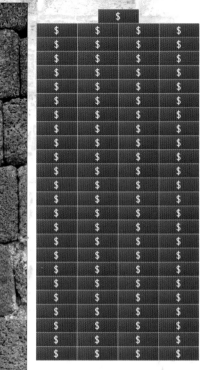

97% of the World's Wealth

POOR

RICH

While the poor majority are surviving on only 3 units of wealth, the rich minority are straining under the weight of 97 units! Perhaps you are wondering which group you are in. If the total value of your home, vehicle, furniture, cash in the bank, and all other assets exceeds $10,000, you are on the wealthy side of this wall.

That's amazing, because if you live in America and have only $10,000 in assets, you might not feel wealthy; in fact, you would probably qualify for some type of government assistance. But because we have been surrounded by masses of other affluent people, we often lose sight of global reality.

Let's look at another reference point often used by economists: Gross Domestic Product. A nation's Gross Domestic Product (GDP) is the total of all goods and services produced in that country.

GDP OF STATE

■ $1 Trillion
■ $300 Billion
■ $100 Billion
■ $100 Billion

Venezuela
Ethiopia
Kenya
Nigeria
Kazakhstan
Myanmar
Tunisia
Uruguay
Ireland
UAE
Sudan
El Salvador
Syria
Thailand
South Korea
Dominican Republic
Bangladesh
Angola
Greece
Ecuador
Vietnam
Saudi Arabia
Israel
Taiwan
Poland
Serbia
Algeria
Austria
Sri Lanka
Finland
Canada
Kuwait
Czech Republic
Hungary
Columbia
South Africa
Philippines
Oman
Puerto Rico
Egypt
Ukraine
Slovakia
Denmark
Mexico
Pakistan
Libya
New Zealand
Switzerland
Belarus
Uzbekistan

[22]

The United States of America has the largest GDP of any country in the world. China is second, but to date, America's GDP is over twice as large as China's. That speaks of an extremely wealthy and productive country!

Some individual states within America have a similar GDP to entire countries. While these numbers fluctuate each year, this map compares the GDP of countries worldwide with individual states.[4]

Notice that California produces more than the entire country of Canada, and Nevada has a similar GDP to Bangladesh. This is even more astounding when you realize that Bangladesh has approximately half the population of the entire United States!

[24]

If America Were a

VILLAGE

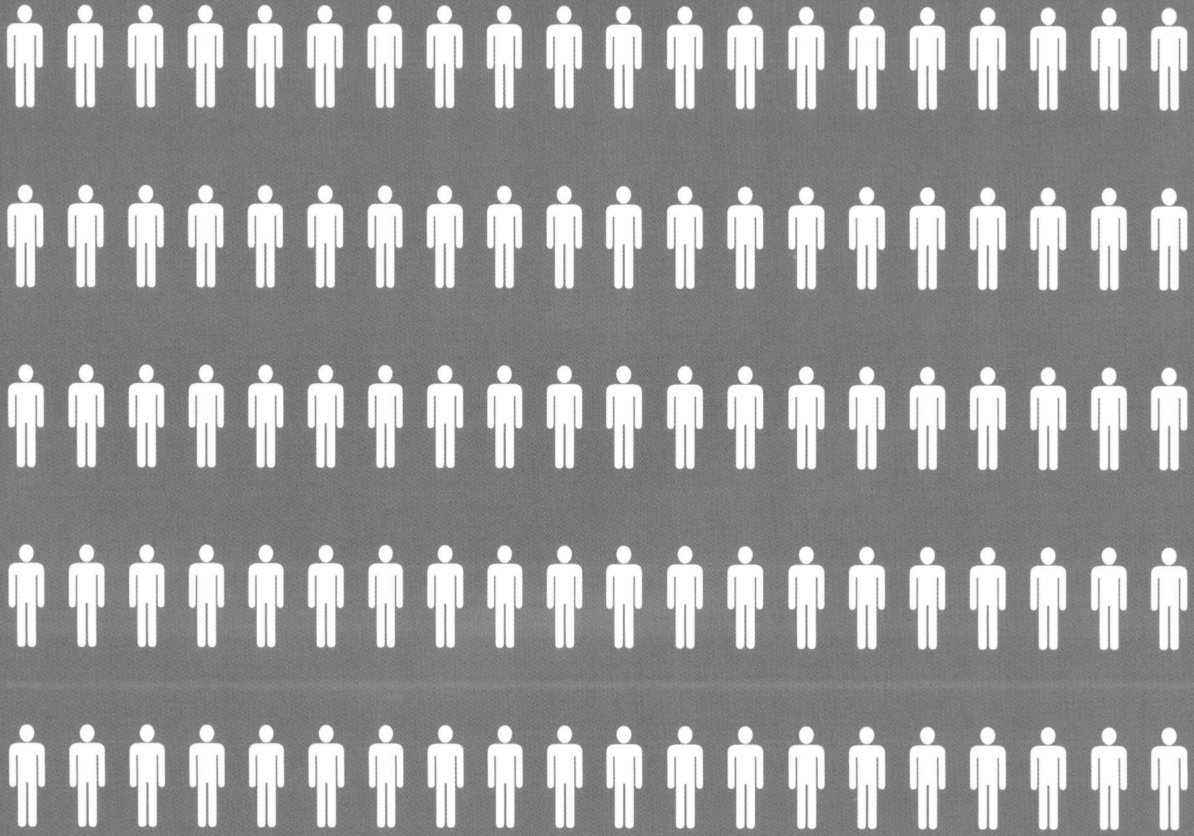

Population by Race

To get a better picture of America's citizens, let's shrink the entire country down to a village of just 100 people. What would the people be like, and what kind of lives would they live?

  For many years America has been a melting pot of nationalities. Many have come to escape persecution or to find a better life economically. Let's begin by looking at the different ethnic races living in America. Each figure on the chart represents about 3.2 million people.

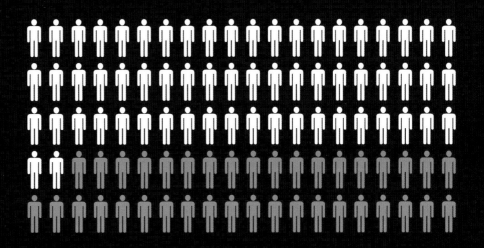

In your American village of 100, 62 citizens would be white. White, or Caucasian, is defined by the United States Census Bureau as a person having origins in any of the original peoples of Europe, the Middle East, or North Africa.

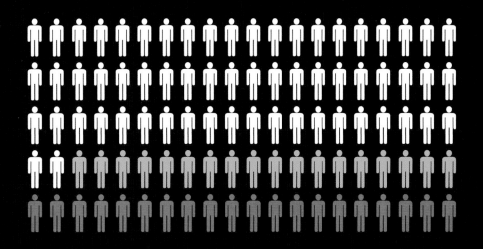

Eighteen in this village would be classified as Hispanic. These are individuals whose family line originated in Spain, but today they may come from Latin America or other Spanish-speaking countries such as the Dominican Republic or Puerto Rico. This is the fastest growing segment in America's population; since 1970 it has grown sixfold.[5]

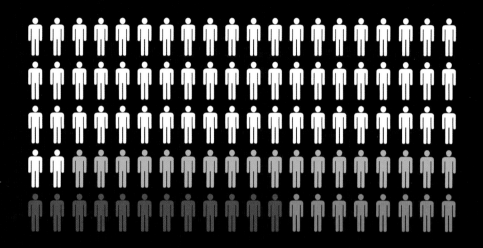

In your village, 12 would classify themselves as African-American. The dictionary defines this group as "Americans who have African and especially black African ancestors."[6] These citizens' family lines come primarily from Sub-Saharan Africa, or the southern portion of the continent.

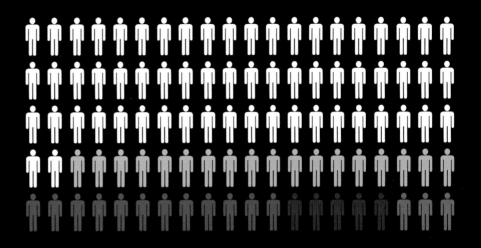

Five in the village would be known as Asian. These people originally
came from Asia, and more specifically, Eastern Asia.

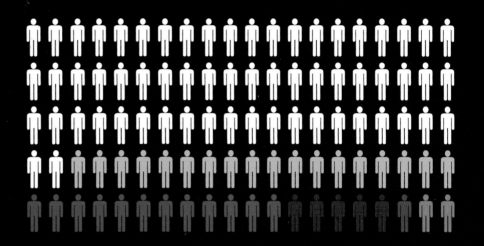

Finally, one of the village citizens would be Native American, and the remaining two would identify themselves as mixed races. While America has always been known for its great diversity in race, the percentage of its citizens born in another country is increasing.

So how many of America's citizens were born in a foreign country?

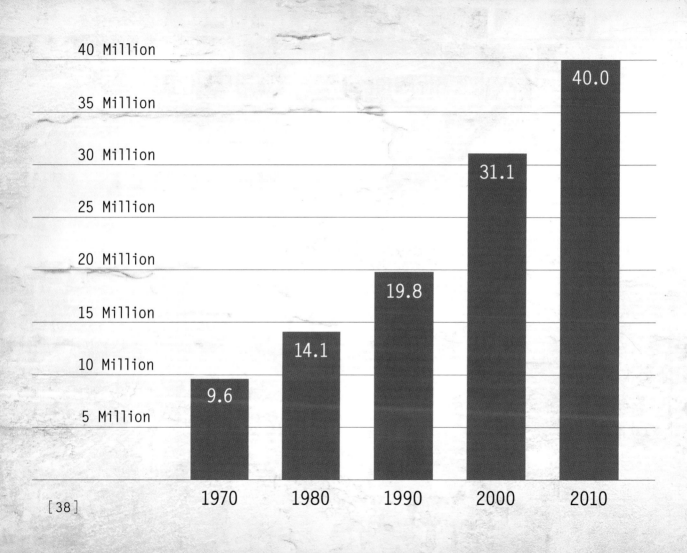

Foreign-Born Population

Today in America the foreign-born population is higher than ever before. Over 40 million people living in the United States were born in another country.[7]

Indeed, 13 people in your village would have been born outside the United States. Many of these arrive unable to speak English, and this puts tremendous pressure on public schools and other government services that must employ translators. Yet it also provides many opportunities to reach out to people from other cultures.

But where in America do all these people live?

City vs. Rural

Eighty-one would live in a city, while only 19 would live in a rural setting. This ratio continues to widen as urban growth in America continues to outpace those moving to the country.

According to the 2013 United States Census Bureau, the New York-Newark metro area is still the nation's most populated area, with 19.9 million people. Los Angeles-Long Beach-Anaheim is second with a population of just over 18 million, and the Chicago area is third with a population of over 8 million.[8]

What kind of housing do all these people live in?

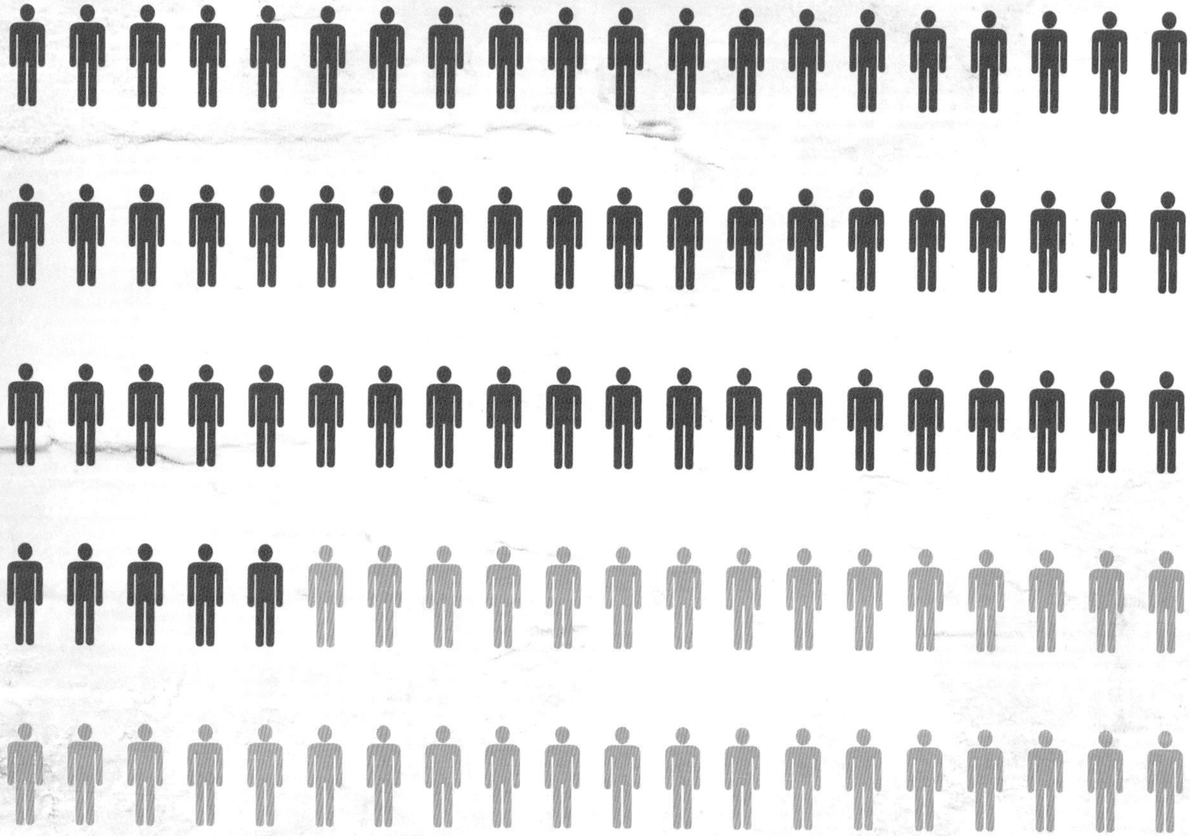

Housing

Sixty-five people in your village would say they own their own home; however, most of them are still making monthly payments. Only 19 of the 65 would own their homes debt-free.[9]

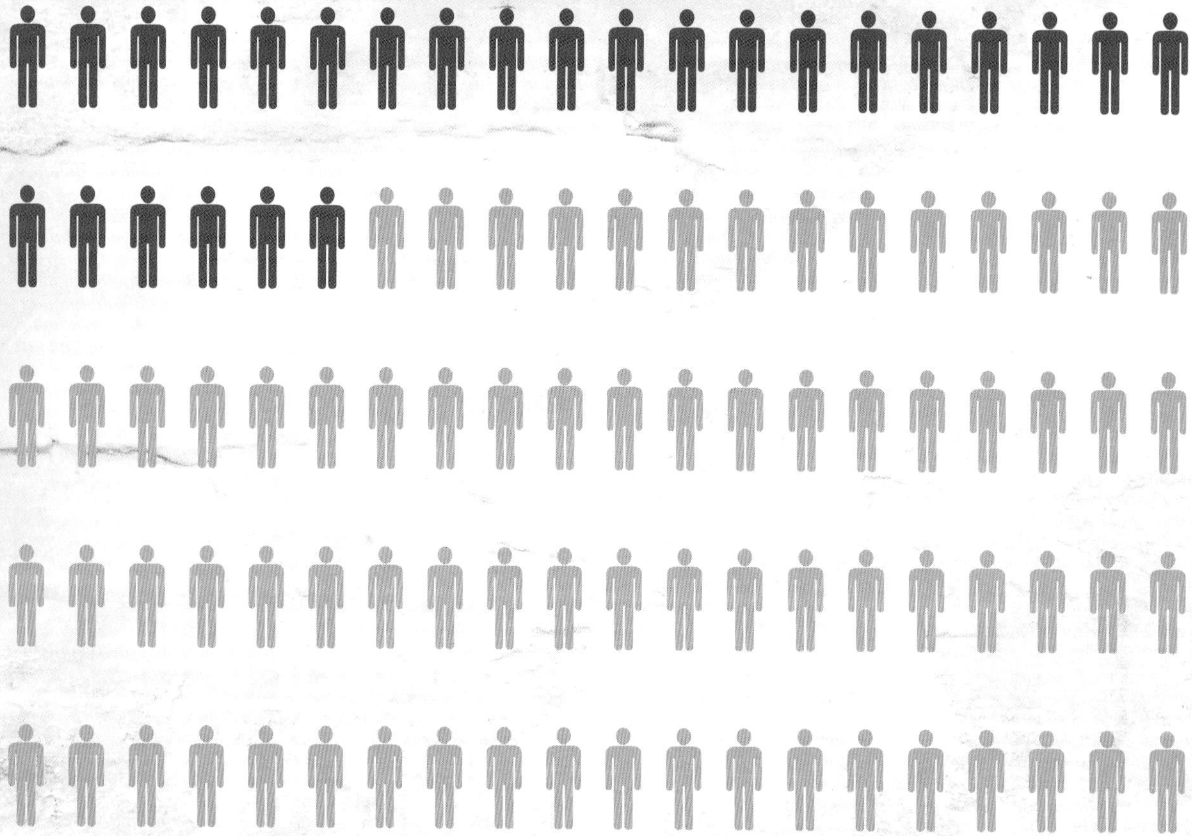

The least expensive housing in America is a multifamily apartment complex, and 26 in your village would live in one of these. Children growing up in these facilities do not have a yard of their own to play in and must use local city parks—if available.

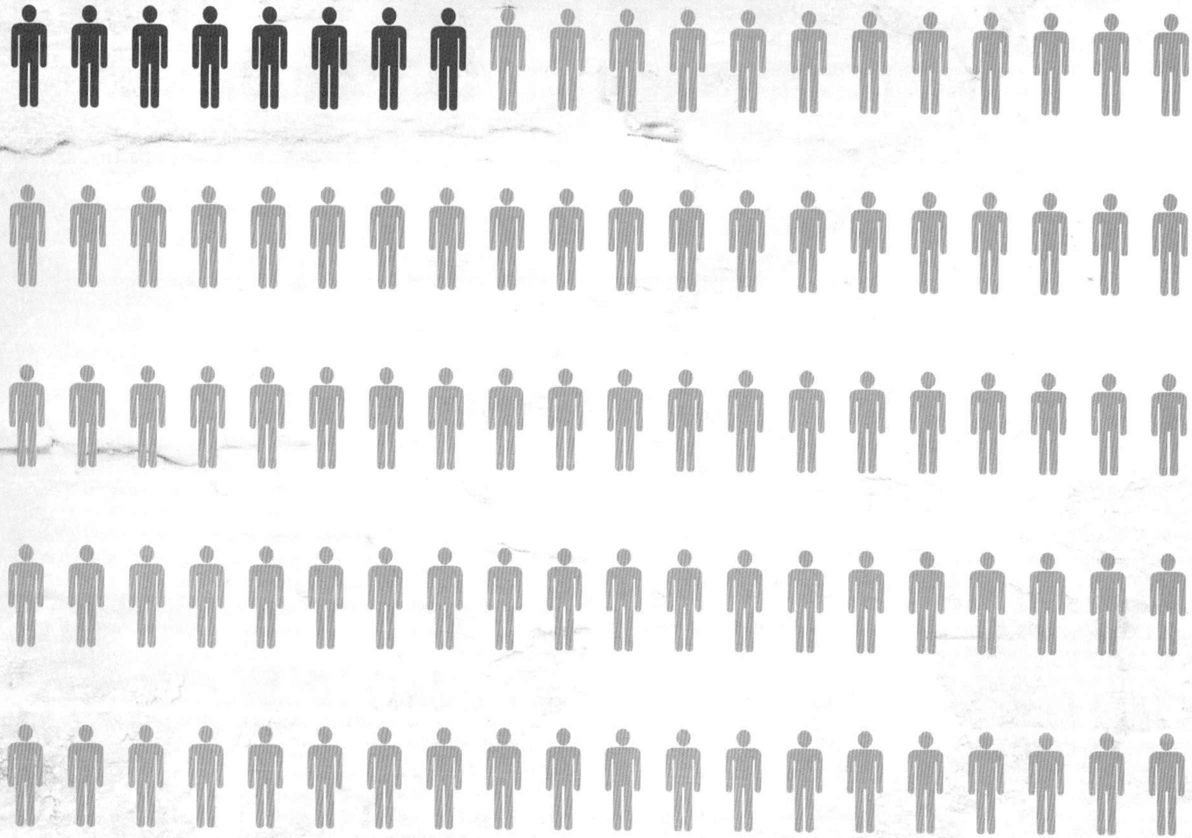

Eight villagers would live in a rented single-family house.

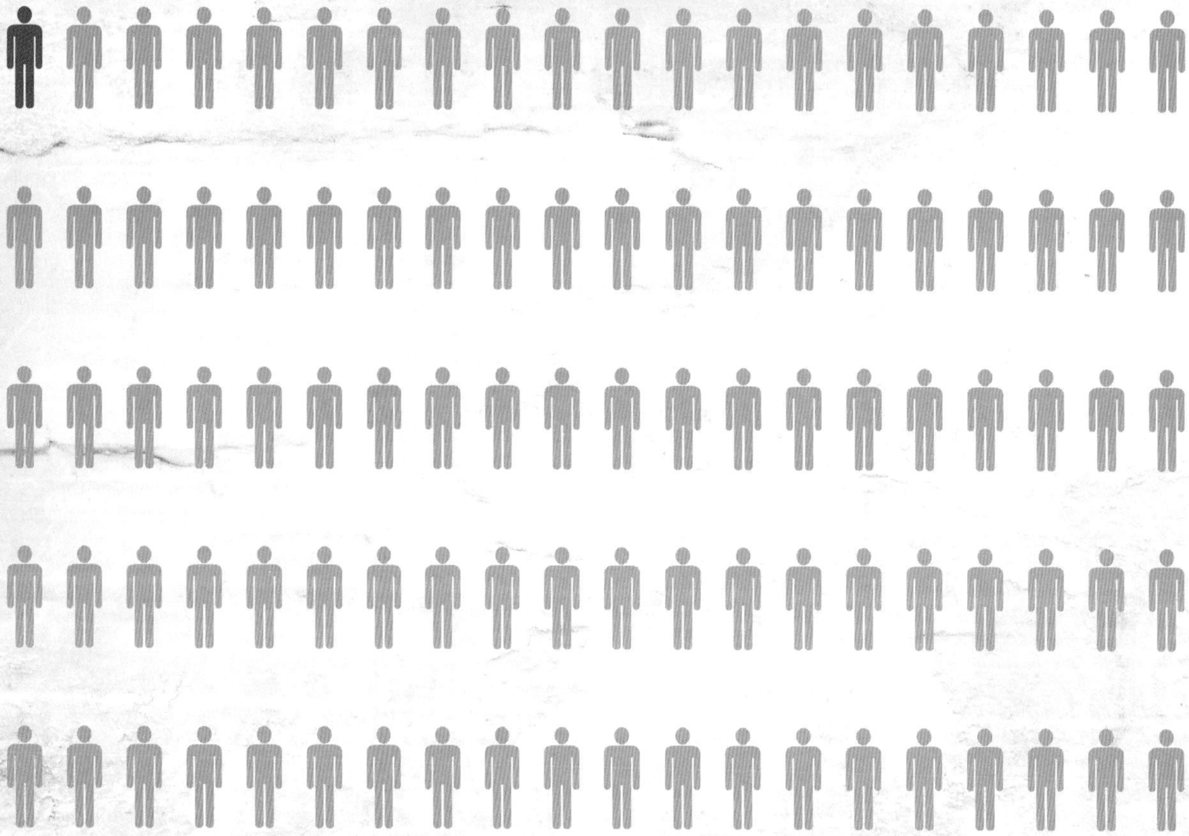

And finally, one in your village would be homeless or have some other housing arrangement.[10]

What about the religious beliefs of the American people?

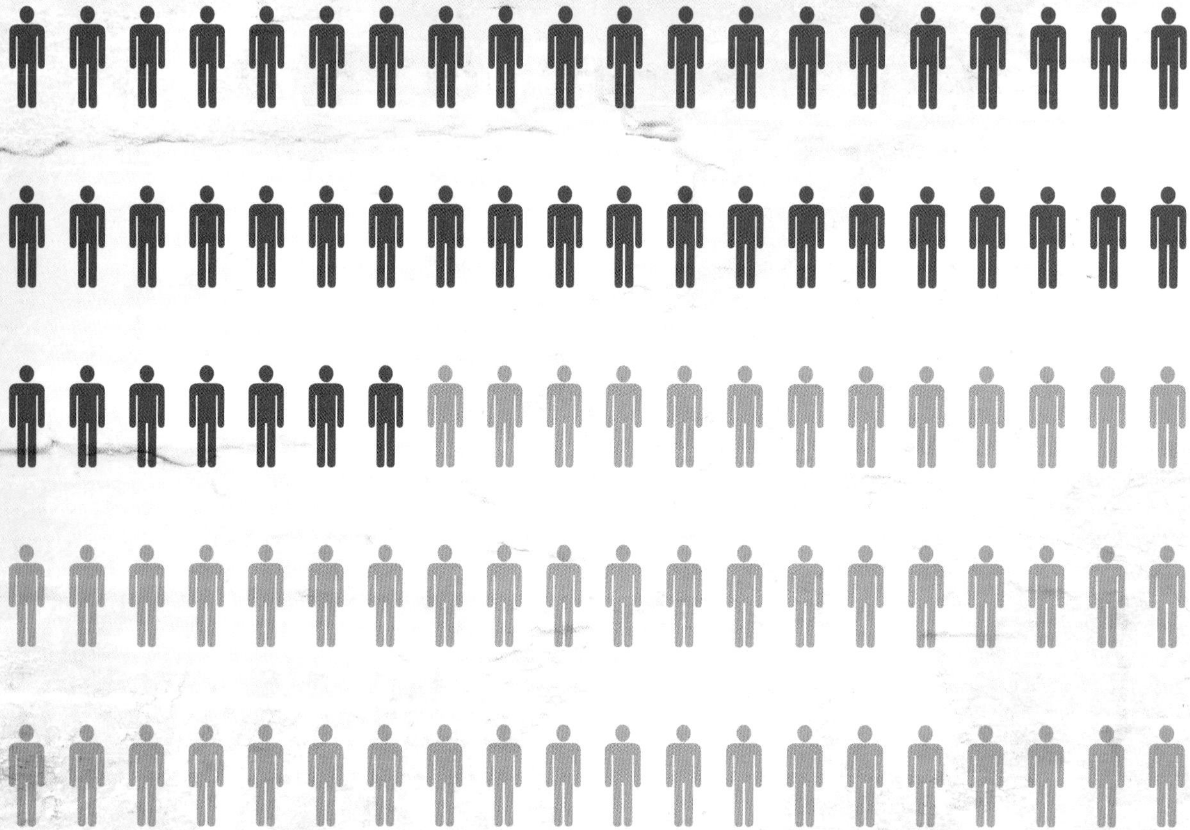

Protestant

Religion

Forty-seven in your village would be known as Christian Protestants. Protestantism originated in the 1500s in reaction to doctrinal differences with the Roman Catholic Church, and today it is the largest religious sector in America. However, in recent years the number of Protestants has been declining.

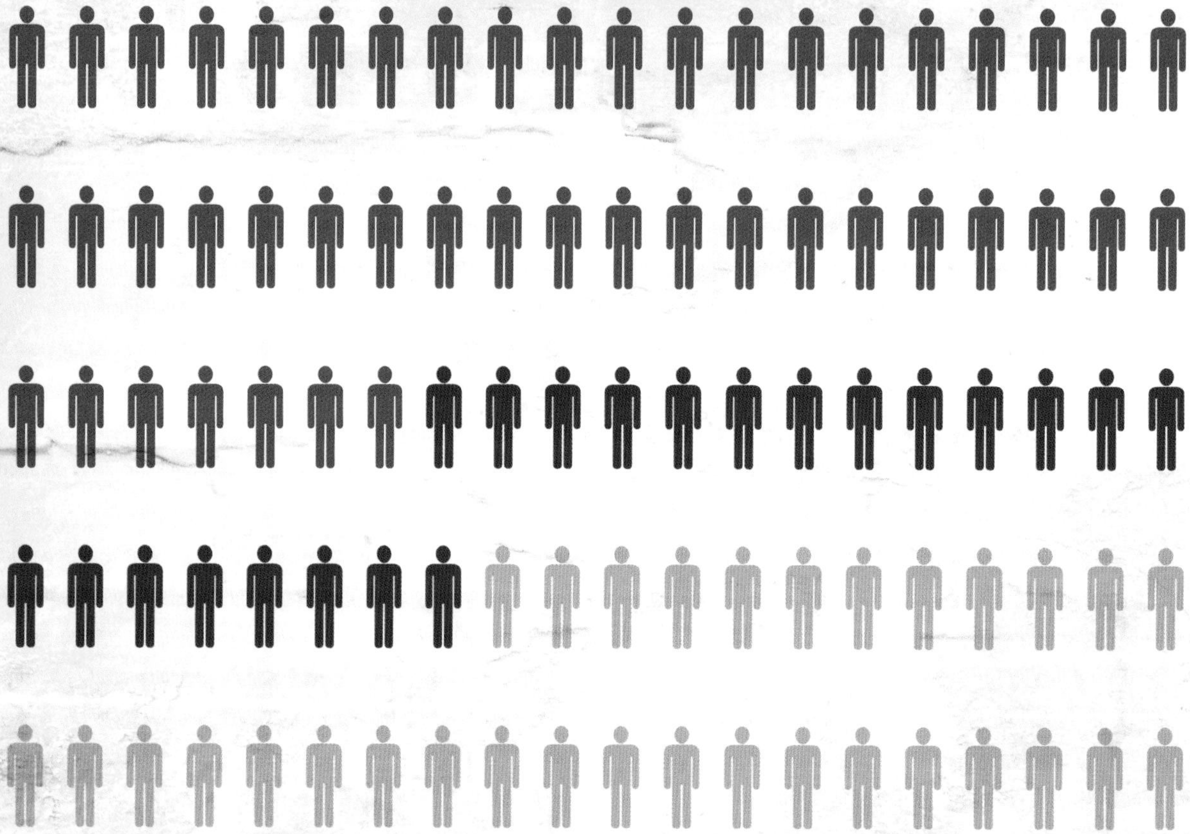

Protestant

Roman
Catholic

Twenty-one in your village would identify themselves as Roman Catholic. This number has remained fairly constant due to a stream of Catholic immigrants replacing the many who have left the Catholic faith over the years. However, in the last decade the overall percentage of people identifying with the Roman Catholic Church in America has been in slow decline.

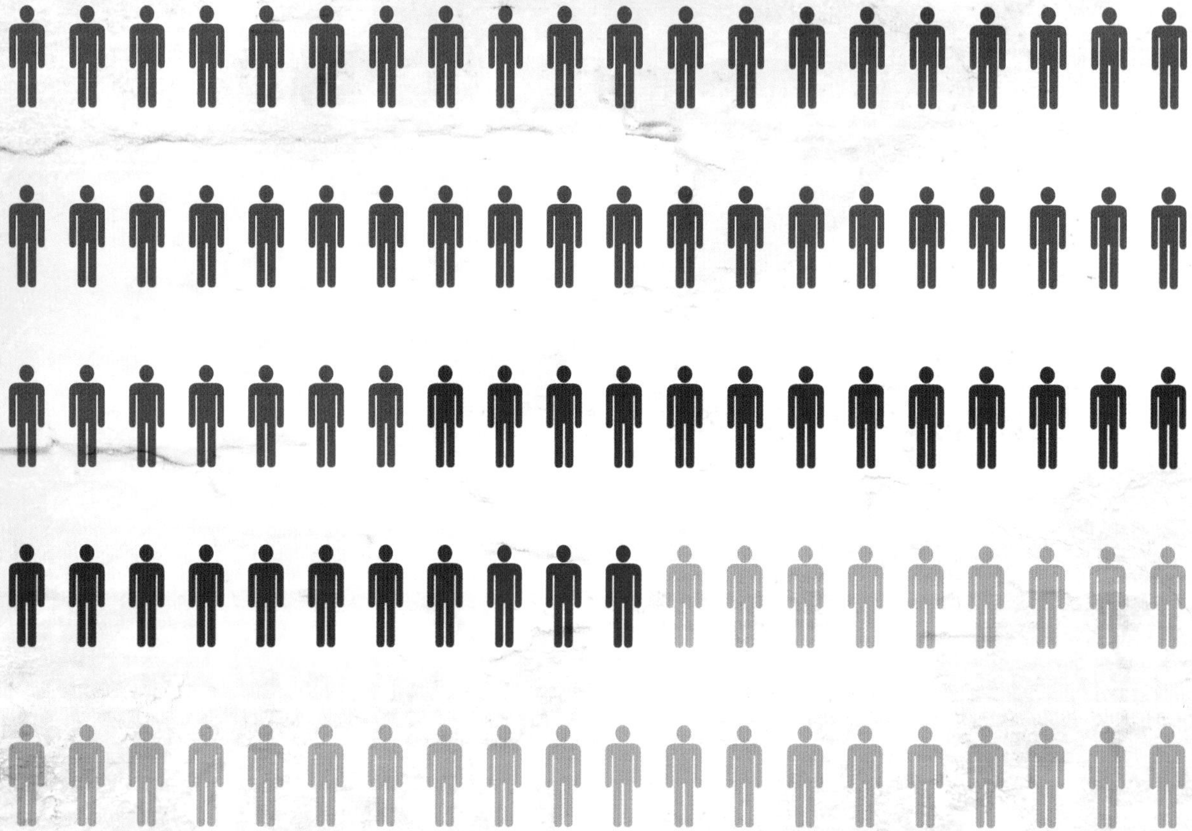

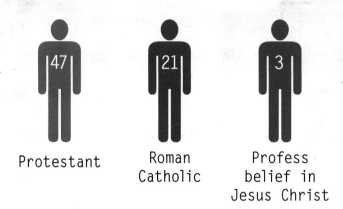

Protestant Roman Catholic Profess belief in Jesus Christ

Three would say they believe in Jesus Christ, but are part of groups like the Mormons, Jehovah's Witnesses, or various other smaller denominations.

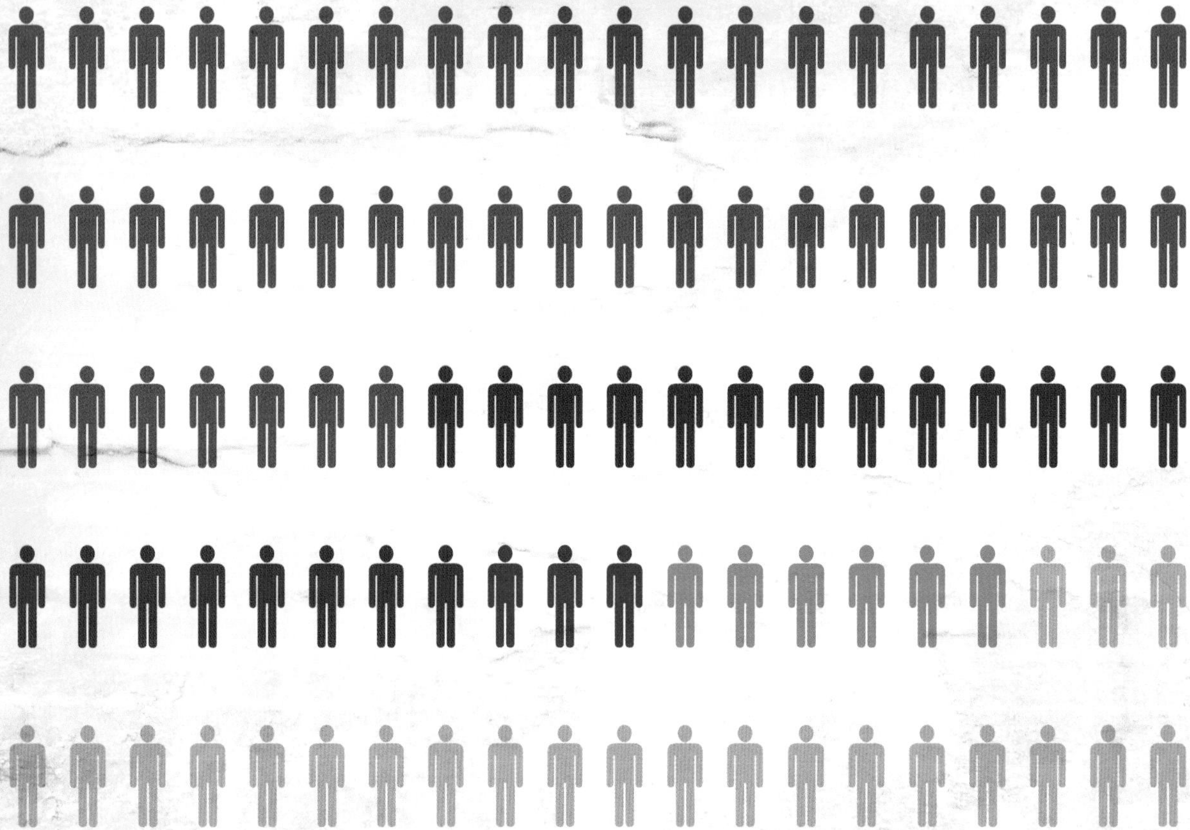

Protestant   Roman Catholic   Profess belief in Jesus Christ   Other religions

Six in your American village would be religious, but would claim faith in something other than Jesus Christ. This would include the Muslims, Hindus, Buddhists, and others. The number in this category has grown recently, particularly as a result of those immigrating to the United States from Middle Eastern countries.

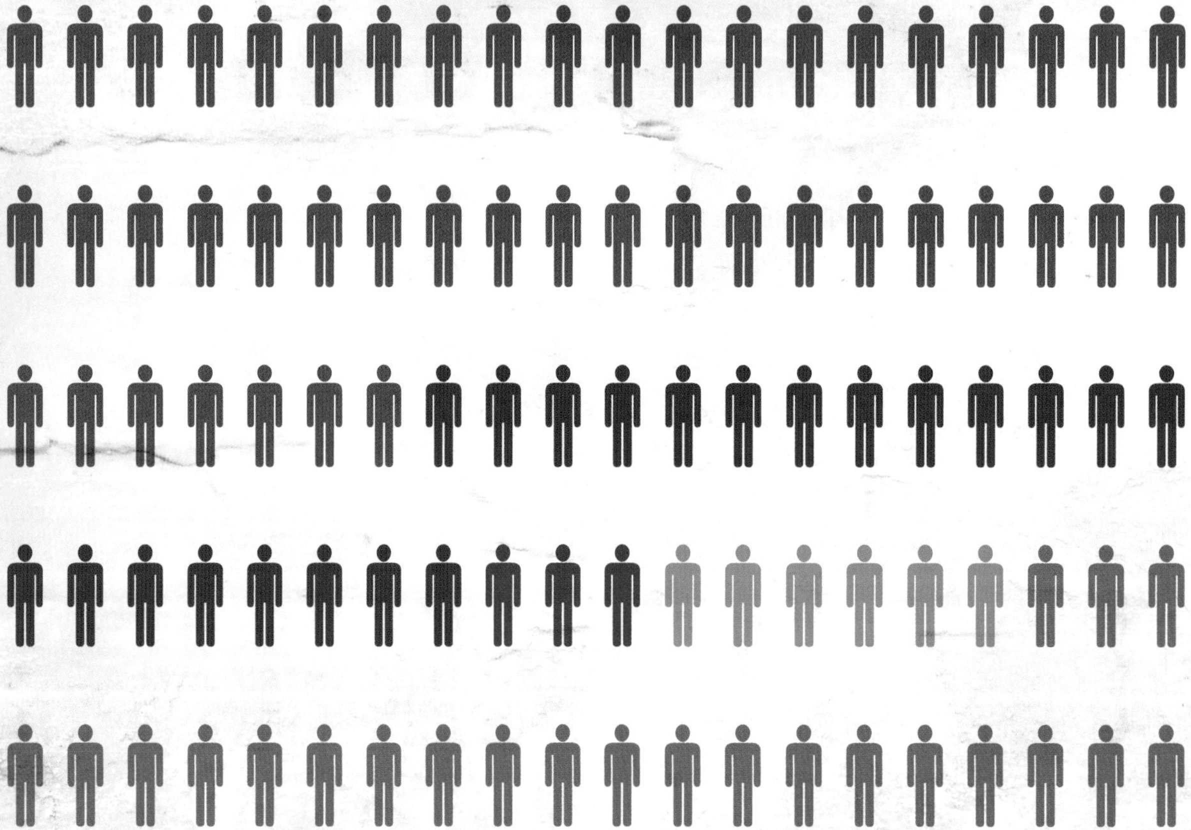

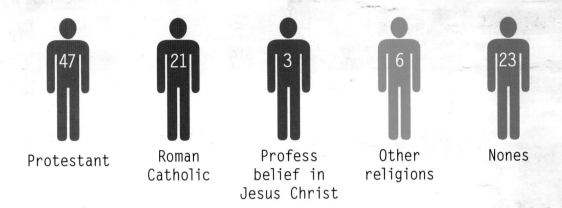

| Protestant | Roman Catholic | Profess belief in Jesus Christ | Other religions | Nones |
| 47 | 21 | 3 | 6 | 23 |

Finally, about 23 in your village would claim no religious affiliation. Sociologists refer to this group as the "Nones," and this is the fastest growing group in America. From 2007 to 2014, this group added about 19 million more to its ranks. These are individuals who have walked away from their faith, the majority coming from the Protestant sector.[11]

So what about the Anabaptist people? How many would live in this village?

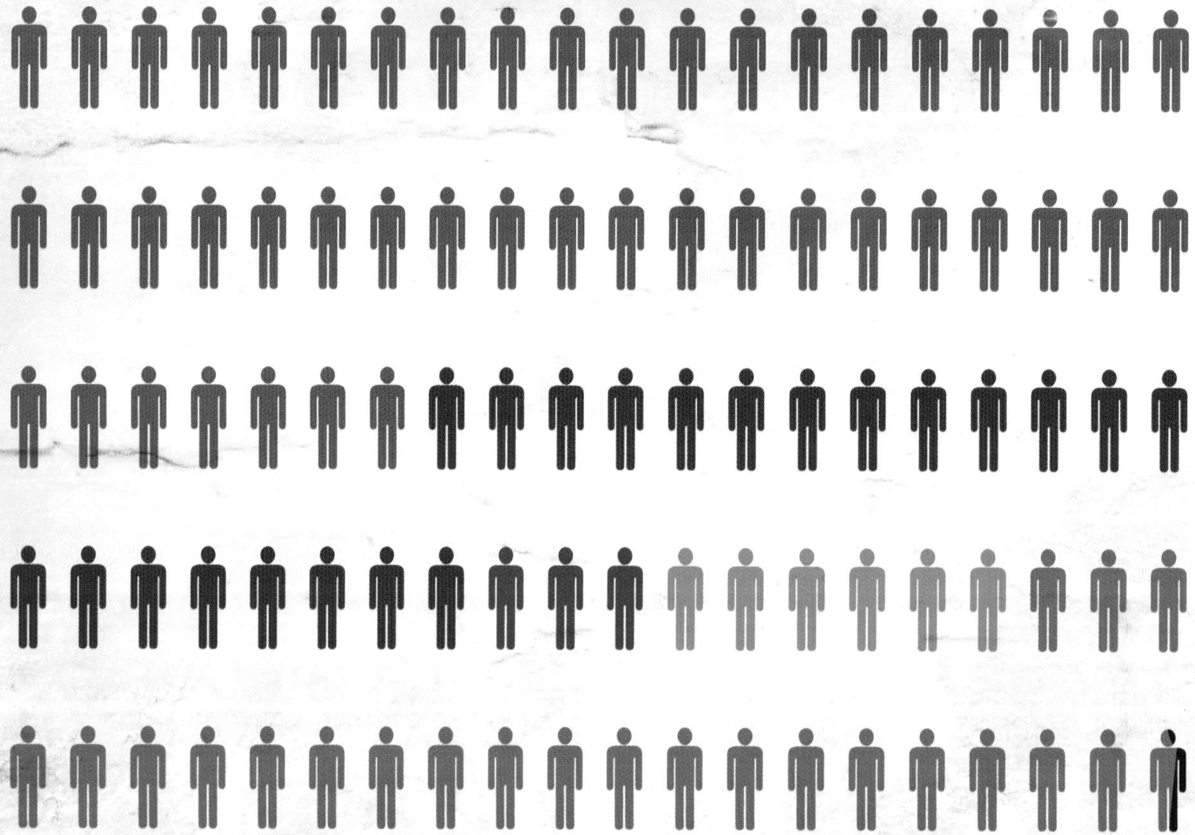

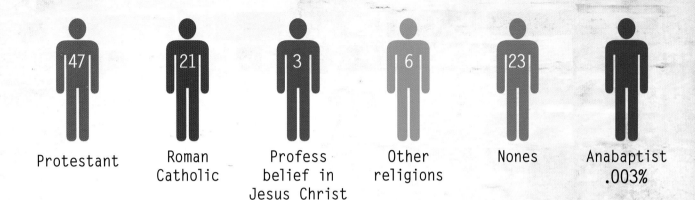

| 47 | 21 | 3 | 6 | 23 | |
| Protestant | Roman Catholic | Profess belief in Jesus Christ | Other religions | Nones | Anabaptist .003% |

Roughly one-third of 1% (.003%) of America claims to be connected to the Anabaptist faith in some way. But let's look closer at the Anabaptist community.[12]

THE ANABAPTIST COMMUNITY

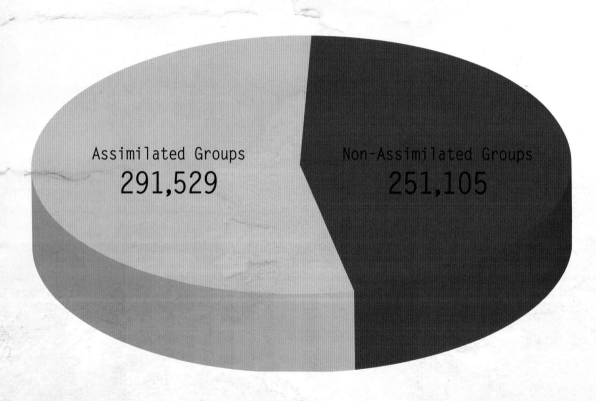

Assimilated Groups
291,529

Non-Assimilated Groups
251,105

There is a wide spectrum within the Anabaptist community, but churches are commonly placed into one of two categories based on how they deal with cultural assimilation in dress. Groups that require their members to dress differently in some way than surrounding society are referred to on the chart as non-assimilated, and those who claim an Anabaptist affiliation yet do not have a specific dress requirement are referred to as assimilated.

A little less than half of the Anabaptist community would be in the non-assimilated category. Sometimes this sector is also referred to as the Plain People. This ratio is changing as the plain, or more conservative groups, have been growing faster than the groups referred to as assimilated.

Let's look a little closer at the more conservative sector of the Anabaptist community in the United States.

PLAIN PEOPLE STATISTICS
(church members)

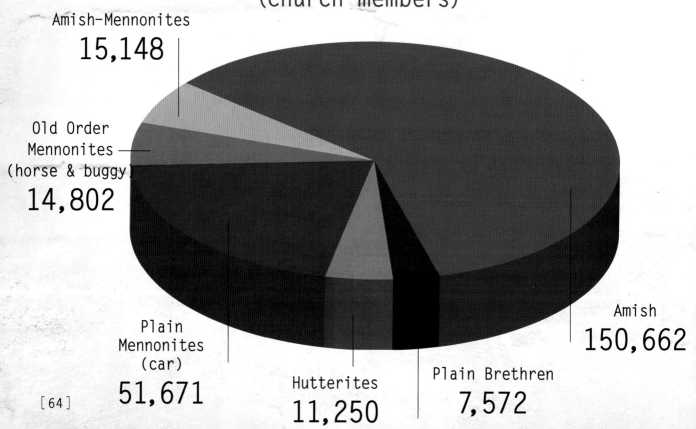

Amish-Mennonites
15,148

Old Order
Mennonites
(horse & buggy)
14,802

Plain
Mennonites
(car)
51,671

Hutterites
11,250

Plain Brethren
7,572

Amish
150,662

By far the largest group within the conservative Anabaptist sector, and the most well known in America, are the Amish.

While there are many differences within these Plain People groups, they are united on some basic fundamentals of Scriptural principle. The most notable and well known is their adherence to Jesus' teaching about defenseless living. All of these groups profess to follow His teachings literally on this topic.[13]

Now let's return to the larger religious community in the United States. Just how many people attend church regularly in America?

40%

Polls taken on the street have been consistent for many years: about 40% of Americans claim to attend church regularly. However, a little investigation reveals something different.

In recent studies where church attendance records rather than public polls were investigated, the percentage of Americans who actually attend church on a regular basis is closer to 18%. This means that on a Sunday morning the majority in your village would be involved in activities other than attending a church service.[14]

This lack of interest in worshiping and seeking God has had a major impact on several areas of our lives, and one of those is our marriages.

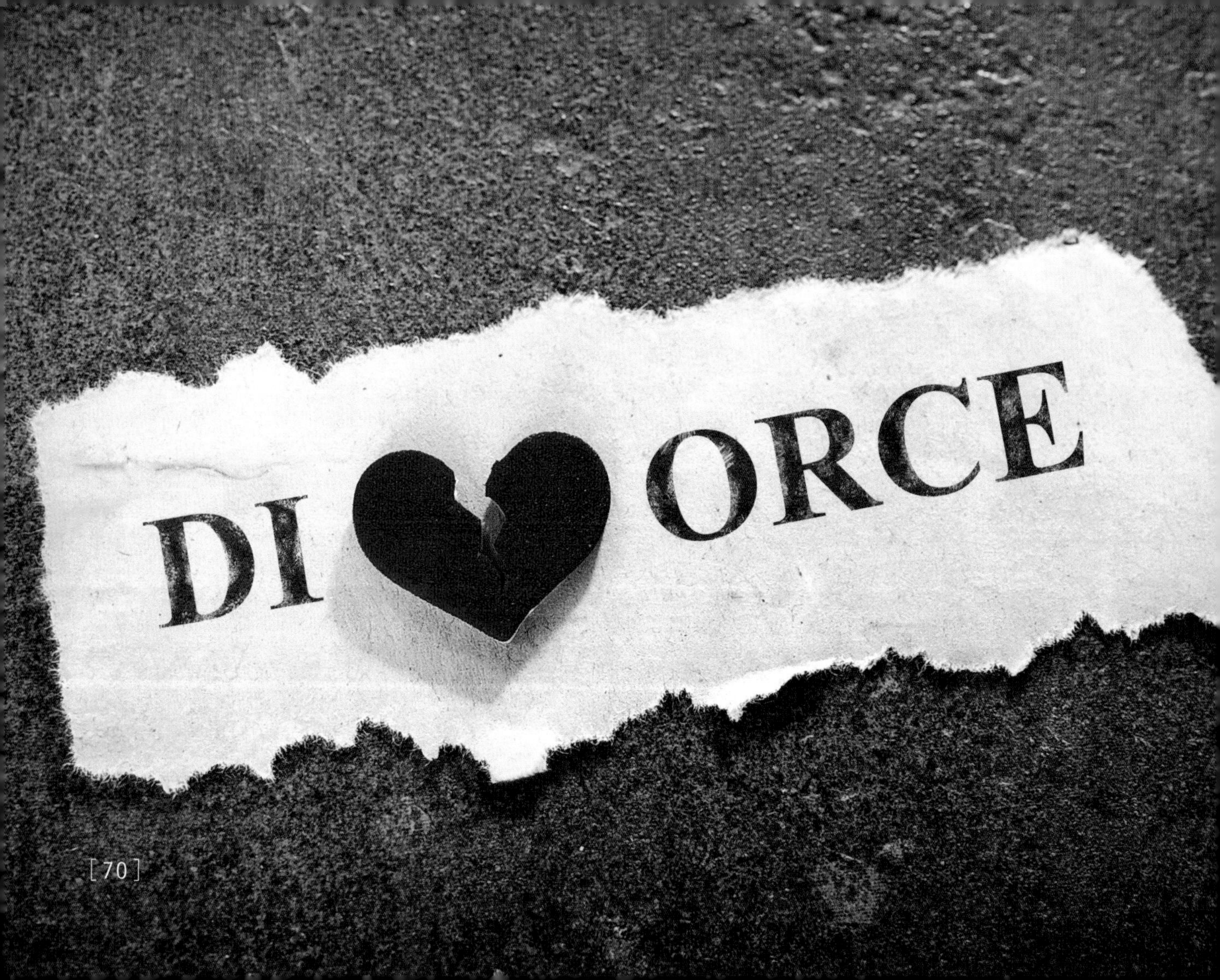
DI ORCE

Divorce Statistics

America has become well known worldwide for its divorce rate. Statistics show that there are about 46,523 divorces in America every week. That computes to one divorce every 13 seconds. And people don't seem to learn from divorce: 41% of first marriages, 60% of second marriages, and 73% of third marriages end in divorce.[15]

This foundational lack of commitment to marriage has had a devastating impact on American home life.

Today, 33% of children in America do not have a father in the home. This is an alarming shift! In 1960 only 11% lived without a father. Today 11% are living in a home without their mother.

This dramatic change has brought many disturbing consequences. Children raised in dysfunctional homes enter life ill-equipped to handle the challenges of daily life. One of the results has been a noticeable upsurge in imprisonments, resulting in increased pressure on America's justice system.[16]

FEDERAL PRISON INCARCERATION RATE

(Number of people incarcerated in federal prison per 100,000 people in country)

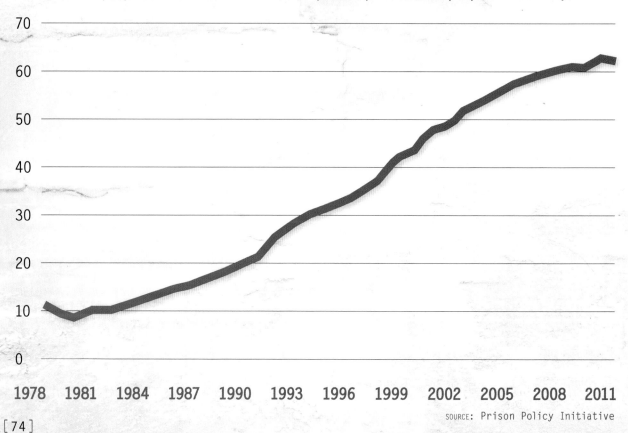

SOURCE: Prison Policy Initiative

Prisoners

This chart shows the increase in federal prisoners per capita over the past decades. There have been occasional fluctuations, but the trend has been upward.[17]

While America has only 5% of the world's population, it has 22% of the world's prisoners. Studies have repeatedly demonstrated that much of this is a result of broken homes in America. But this is just one effect of America's dysfunctional home life.[18]

Let's look at another area where unstructured home life is affecting America.

Meals

At one time almost every family in America sat down at regular times to eat meals together. But over the last century this has changed. Today in many homes, few meals are eaten together, and these meals are often something prepackaged from the freezer and consumed in front of the television. Lives are busy and schedules difficult to synchronize, and many have resorted to grabbing something from one of the many fast food restaurants in town. Where at one time eating out was a treat, today about half of America's meals are eaten away from home. And as America has increasingly dined away from home, something else has increased as well—calorie consumption.[19]

Let's look at how the United States compares with other countries in calories consumed per day.

4,000 calories	
3,500 calories	
3,000 calories	
2,500 calories	
2,000 calories	
1,500 calories	1,590
1,000 calories	

Congo

Daily Calorie Consumption

The Republic of Congo, located in Central Africa, has a population of about 70 million people. Their diet consists of maize, rice, cassava (manioc), sweet potatoes, yam, plantain, tomatoes, pumpkins, and varieties of peas and nuts. Their average calorie consumption per day is 1,590.

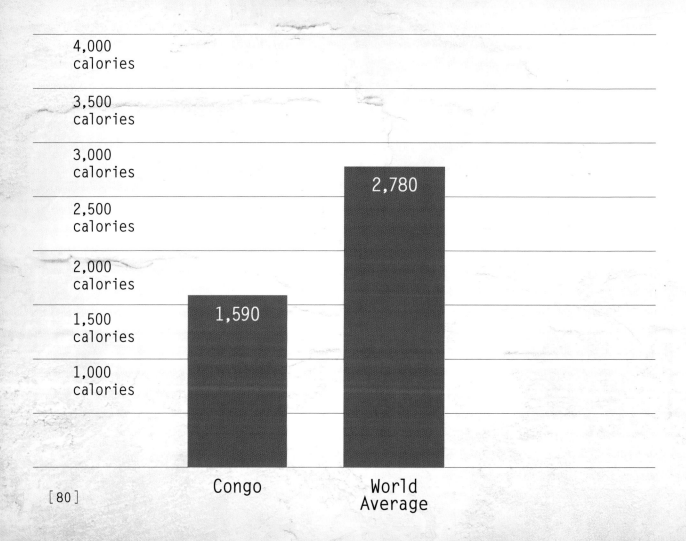

4,000 calories	
3,500 calories	
3,000 calories	
	2,780
2,500 calories	
2,000 calories	
1,500 calories	1,590
1,000 calories	
	Congo · World Average

If you average the calorie intake of every country in the world, you will find that the average person consumes about 2,780 calories each day. This number has been gradually increasing. In 1965 the average calorie intake was just over 2,300 calories per day.[20]

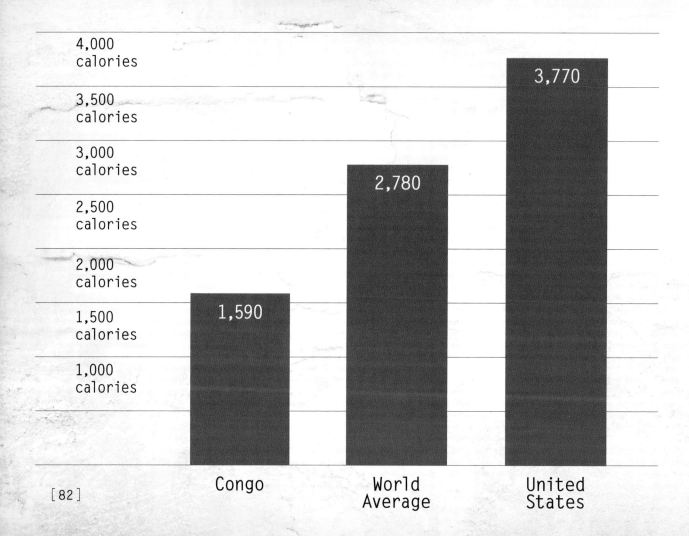

		4,000 calories				3,770
		3,500 calories				
		3,000 calories		2,780		
		2,500 calories				
		2,000 calories				
		1,500 calories	1,590			
		1,000 calories				

Congo   World Average   United States

But America consumes much more. It is estimated that the average American consumes 3,770 calories per day. This has had a profound effect on our health, and the medical community and even the government are concerned. In 1928, having enough food was such a primary concern that Herbert Hoover won a landslide election to the presidency by offering "a chicken in every pot."[21] But times have changed. Doctors today are more concerned about the rise in calorie consumption than about everyone getting enough chicken.

But they are concerned not only about the growing calorie intake. Something else is on the rise in America.

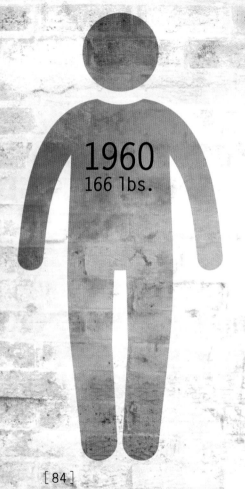

1960
166 lbs.

Body Weight

Body weight is increasing. In 1960 the average American male tipped the scales at 166 pounds. People were more active in those years and had less prepared and processed food.

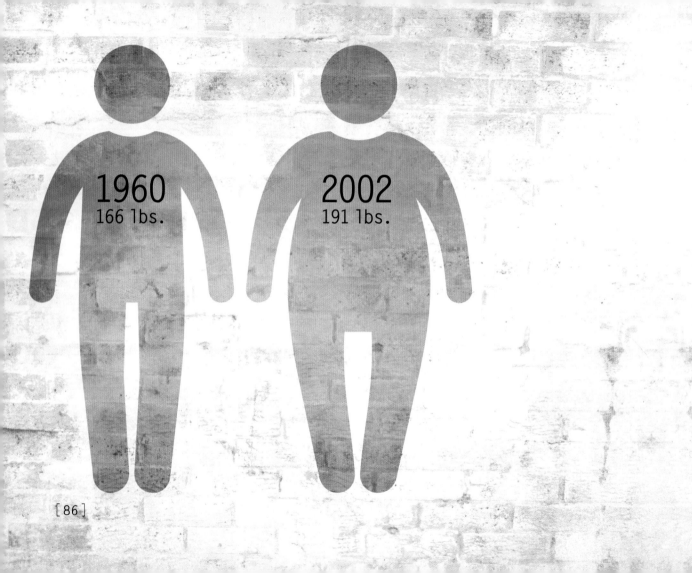

1960
166 lbs.

2002
191 lbs.

By 2002 the average man had increased to 191 pounds, and many were voicing concern.[22]

Even airlines have been impacted. On June 26, 2002, Southwest Airlines enacted a policy requiring overweight passengers to purchase two tickets. One study estimated that airlines spent $275 million per year for every 10 pounds of increased weight per passenger, since the added weight increases fuel consumption.[23]

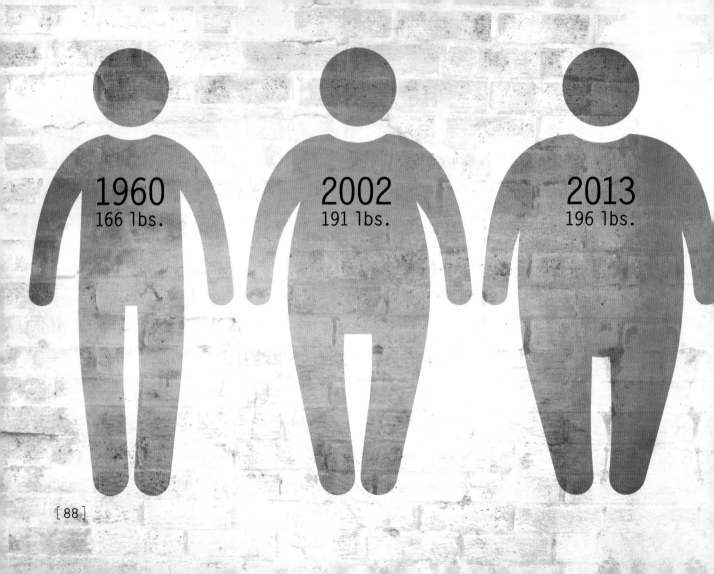

1960
166 lbs.

2002
191 lbs.

2013
196 lbs.

Today the average American male is approaching 200 pounds.

It is interesting that in 1990 no state within America reported an obesity rate greater than 14%. Just ten years later, 23 states reported an obesity rate of 20% to 24%. But by 2010, 36 states reported an obesity rate of at least 25%, and 12 states were reporting an obesity rate beyond 30%.[24]

So what would all this look like in your village of 100?

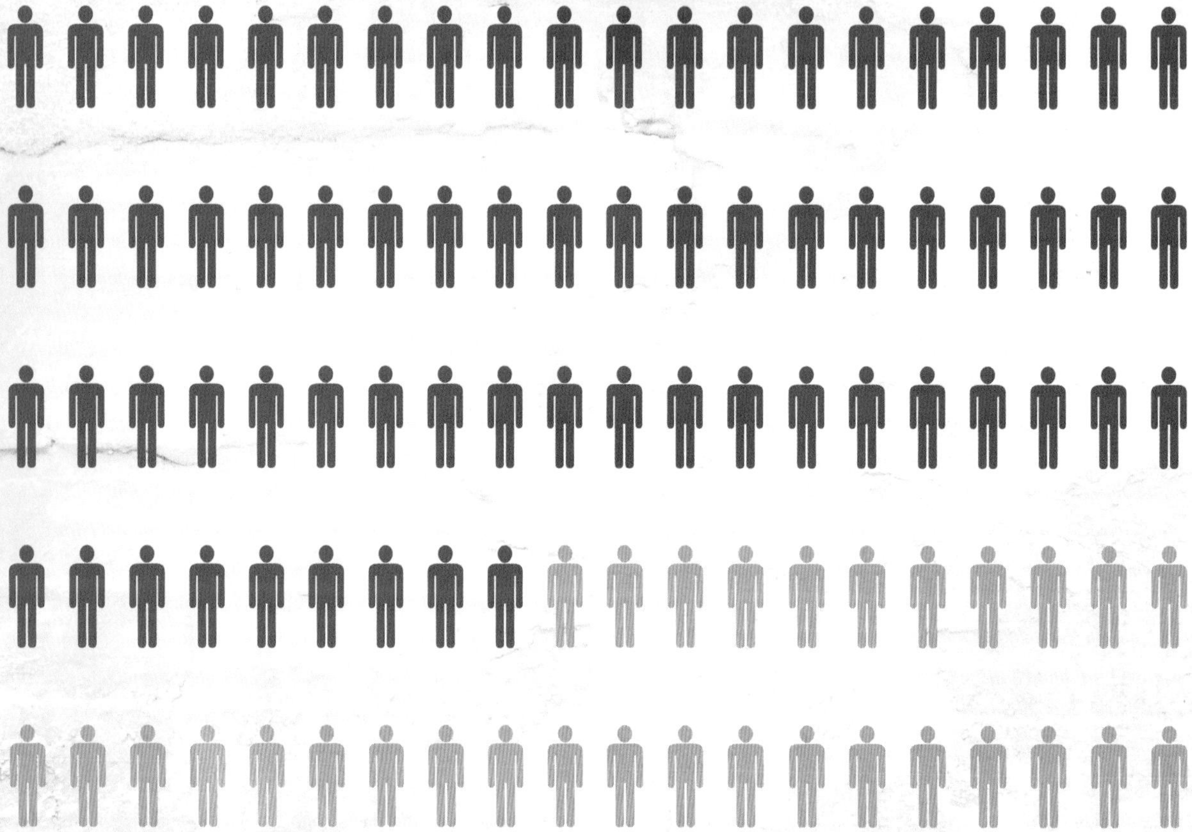

Around 69 would be considered overweight or obese by the medical community. This statistic has alarmed many medical researchers, with some warning that obesity is the single greatest threat to the nation's future.[25]

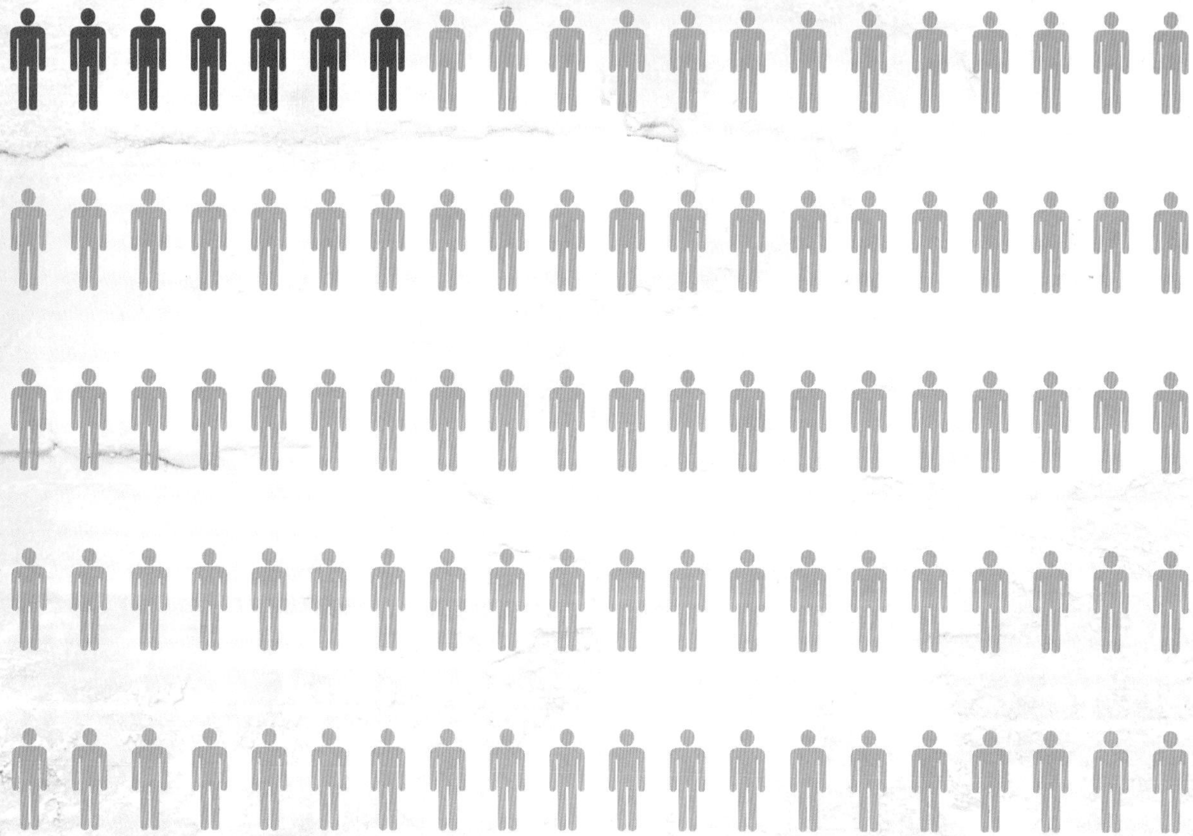

Seven in your village would be severely overweight, or roughly 100 pounds too heavy. This means around 20 million Americans would fit in this category.[26]

But the strangest thing is that it is the "American poor" who are most affected by obesity. Throughout history, and in many countries today, being overweight is a sign of wealth. After all, only the rich in many cultures can afford to eat more than they need. But in this place called America it is very different.[27]

This is partly due to inexpensive food. The amazing fact is that though American food consumption is at an all-time high, our food costs are at an all-time low.

In other words, even though we are eating more, it is costing us less!

And having

FOOD AND RAIMENT

let us be therewith

CONTENT.

—1 Timothy 6:8

The Apostle Paul told Timothy that "having food and raiment let us be therewith content." But how much money does it take for a person to be content, and how has this changed over the years?

Let's go back and look at how expensive food and clothing were in the past, and then compare the cost to America today.

1914
% OF HOUSEHOLD BUDGET

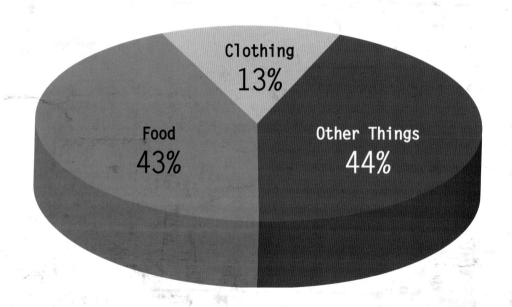

Clothing
13%

Food
43%

Other Things
44%

Food and Clothes

A hundred years ago, the average American spent about 43% of his paycheck on food. Food was a major cost in his budget. 13% of his money went to purchase clothing for his family. This left only 44% of his paycheck to cover housing, transportation, and all the other things required to make a household function.[28]

  This means there wasn't a lot of money left over for luxuries or even for things we might regard as necessities today.

2014
% OF HOUSEHOLD BUDGET

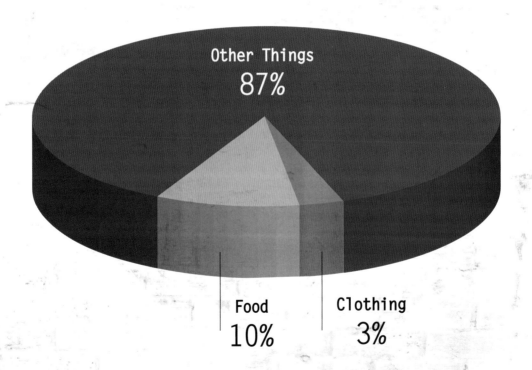

Other Things
87%

Food
10%

Clothing
3%

Today the average American's financial life is much different. Only about 10% is spent on food, largely due to new agricultural technology and inexpensive food shipped in from less affluent countries.[29]

Clothing is also much cheaper, but again, this is largely because most of what we wear is made outside of the country by individuals who work hard and receive little for their effort.

Notice how much of the average American's paycheck, compared to a hundred years ago, is available for items beyond food and clothing.

But have you ever wondered how food costs in America compare with other nations?

SPENDING ON FOOD

Selected countries, 2011, % of total household spending

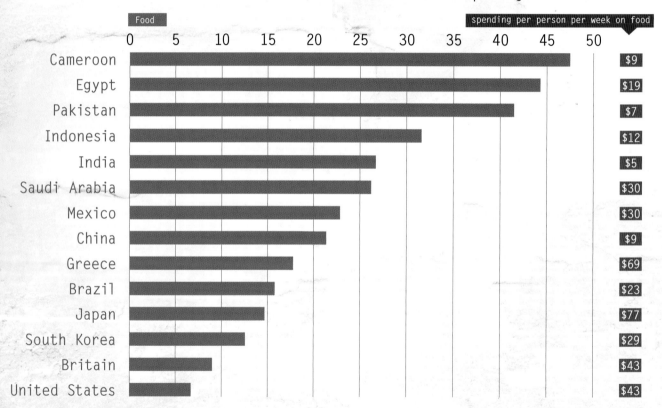

	Food (% of total household spending)	spending per person per week on food
Cameroon	47	$9
Egypt	44	$19
Pakistan	42	$7
Indonesia	31	$12
India	27	$5
Saudi Arabia	26	$30
Mexico	23	$30
China	21	$9
Greece	18	$69
Brazil	16	$23
Japan	14	$77
South Korea	13	$29
Britain	9	$43
United States	6	$43

SOURCE: US Department of Agriculture

We seldom give much thought to the amazingly low food costs in America as compared to other countries. This chart compares numerous countries and the difference in percentage of household income spent on food and drink. America spends just a fraction of what many countries spend on food.[30]

So where is all the extra money going in America? Let's look at a few places this extra money tends to go.

60 billion

Ways America Spends Its Extra Money

Americans spend roughly $60 billion on their **pets** per year. While a little over a third of this is on pet food, costs related to grooming, boarding, training, and pet-sitting have also rapidly increased. Americans are aging, and many are turning to pets to fill the void in their homes and lives as children move away.[31]

Soft drinks, at one time a rare treat, today have become a "necessity" for many. Americans spend over $65 billion each year on soft drinks.[32]

11

billion

Eleven billion is spent on bottled water. This is an amazing phenomenon that our grandparents could never have predicted. Most tap water in America is very safe, yet people like the convenience of bottled water.

In recent years ecologists have been asking pointed questions regarding the wisdom of this trend. They argue that bottled water is damaging our environment, noting that fossil fuel is used to make the bottles and transport the product, greenhouse gases are emitted, and the plastic containers end up in American landfills.

40 billion

Americans spend around $40 billion each year on their **lawns.** Believe it or not, it costs more to maintain an acre of American lawn than it does to grow an acre of corn, rice, or sugarcane in many countries.[33]

Americans spend $5.8 billion each year keeping their vehicles clean.[34]

10 billion

Over $10 billion is spent on romance novels.

And an estimated $65 billion is spent each year on recreational hunting and fishing. There's seemingly no end to the number of items "needed" to make these pastimes more enjoyable. American people can be very passionate about hunting and fishing. But $65 billion is a lot of money.[35]

Pets $60 Billion

Soft Drinks $65 Billion

Bottled Water $11 Billion

Lawn Care $40 Billion

Car Washes $5.8 Billion

Romance Novels $10 Billion

Hunting/Fishing $65 Billion

As you look over this list, it is obvious that Americans are spending a lot of money on nonessentials.

So why does all of this matter?

Money equals

OPPORTUNITY,

and money squandered equals

OPPORTUNITY LOST

How many opportunities are being lost, and what could this much money accomplish if some of it were used differently?

What if some of this money were diverted to assist people with real needs around the globe?

While sustainable change takes more than just money, let's look at some estimates aid organizations have proposed.

10 billion

It is estimated that just $10 billion in additional funding could provide clean drinking water for every person on the globe. Compare this amount to what America is currently spending each year on bottled water.[36]

26 billion

The additional funding needed to educate every child on the globe is estimated to be around $26 billion.[37]

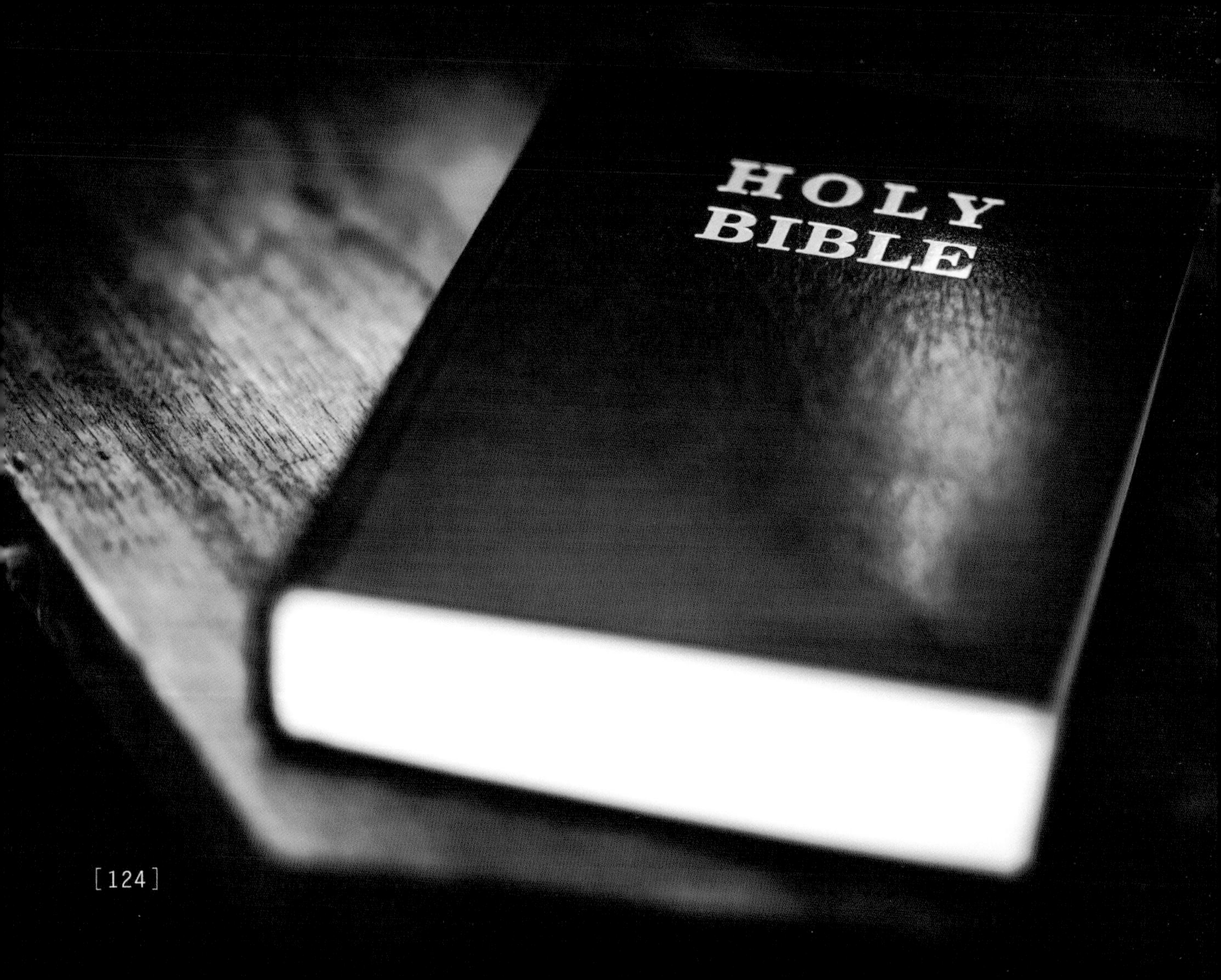
HOLY
BIBLE

11 billion

And while unfortunately not everyone wants one, a new Bible could be provided to every person on the earth for around $11 billion.

It is amazing how much Americans spend on nonessentials when compared to how little it takes to help the needy. Americans have been given many resources and much opportunity.

So how much money is actually going from these wealthy Americans to those in great need?

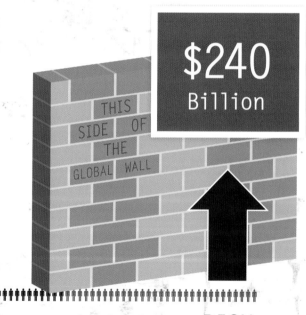

POOR

RICH

Charitable Giving

Americans are known to be very charitable people, and it is estimated
that they give approximately $240 billion to charitable organizations
each year. That is a tremendous amount of money. Where does that
money go? [38]

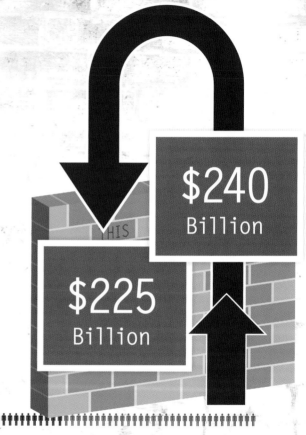

$240 Billion

THIS

$225 Billion

POOR

RICH

Almost all of this private charitable giving remains with people living in America. It builds private schools for their children, gymnasiums for their churches, and in many ways improves their own lives in America.

So how much actually goes over the wall to the poor living in developing countries?

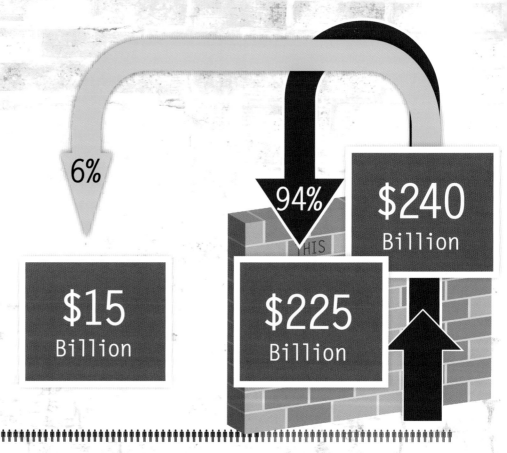

PERCENTAGE
WHICH
GOES TO
DEVELOPING
COUNTRIES

6%

94%

$15
Billion

$225
Billion

$240
Billion

POOR

RICH

An estimated $15 billion, only a little over 6% of America's total private charitable giving, goes over the wall and is used to improve the lives of people within developing countries.[39]

PERCENTAGE OF INCOME SHARED BY DEVELOPED COUNTRIES

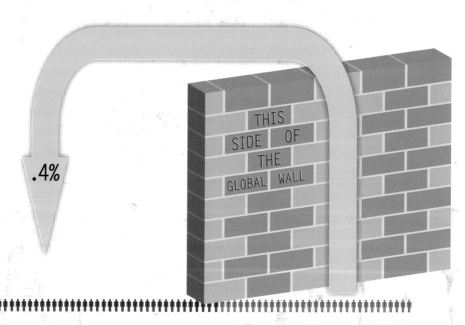

.4%

THIS
SIDE OF
THE
GLOBAL WALL

POOR

RICH

In fact, it is estimated that the total aid sent to developing countries equals only 0.4% of the combined national income of developed countries. Those of us living on the wealthy side spend more on our pets than we share with the poor.[40]

THIS
SIDE OF
THE
GLOBAL WALL

There is tremendous disparity in our world. While some have difficulty finding food for the day, others have too much and struggle with obesity. We have looked at America and its people. We've seen how they spend their great wealth and how much they share. But we need to remember that this disparity hasn't always been so vast, and we forget the great opportunities of our time.

It is important that we consider not only the extreme wastefulness of America, but also the uniqueness of the time we live in.

Have you ever considered how unusual our time is from a historical perspective?

The Uniqueness of Our
TIME

We live in an
unprecedented time
with unparalleled
opportunity!

When faced with some of the facts we have reviewed, it is easy to spiral into negativity and condemnation of ourselves and others. We can begin to focus on human sinfulness and American self-centeredness, spending our time mentally castigating others for not sharing more. In doing this, we can totally miss an even more powerful reality.

We live in an unprecedented time with unparalleled opportunity!

Let's look at some historical facts to get a picture of what God might have in mind, beginning with changes in world population.

1 BILLION PEOPLE

?

| 4000 BC | 3800 BC | 3600 BC | 3400 BC | 3200 BC | 3000 BC | 2800 BC | 2600 BC | 2400 BC | 2200 BC | 2000 BC | 1800 BC | 1600 BC | 1400 BC | 1200 BC | 1000 BC | 800 BC | 600 BC | 400 BC | 33 AD | 400 AD | 600 AD | 800 AD | 1000 AD | 1200 AD | 1400 AD | 1600 AD | 1800 AD | 2015 AD |

World Population

This is a timeline from Creation to now, with the gray line starting around the time of Noah's Flood. It is estimated that when Jesus said the fields were white already to harvest, there were only around 200 million people on the entire globe.[41]

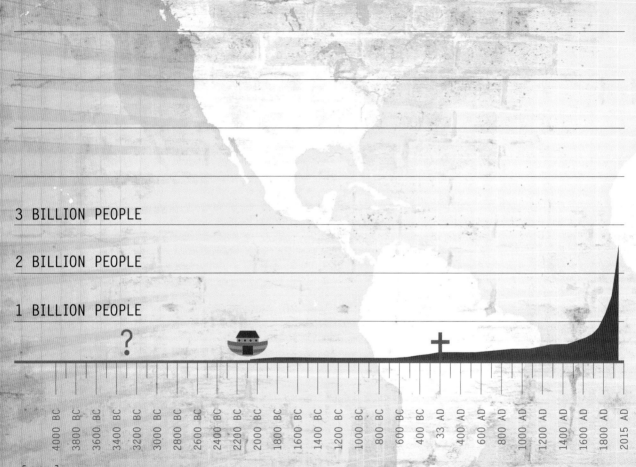

3 BILLION PEOPLE

2 BILLION PEOPLE

1 BILLION PEOPLE

?

4000 BC 3800 BC 3600 BC 3400 BC 3200 BC 3000 BC 2800 BC 2600 BC 2400 BC 2200 BC 2000 BC 1800 BC 1600 BC 1400 BC 1200 BC 1000 BC 800 BC 600 BC 400 BC 33 AD 400 AD 600 AD 800 AD 1000 AD 1200 AD 1400 AD 1600 AD 1800 AD 2015 AD

1750
770 MILLION

1950
2.5 BILLION

By 1750, just before the Revolutionary War here in America, the world had grown to about 770 million inhabitants. On the graph you will see that growth up to this time was slow and fairly consistent.

But by 1950, just 200 years later, the population had exploded to 2.5 billion people. What a huge jump!

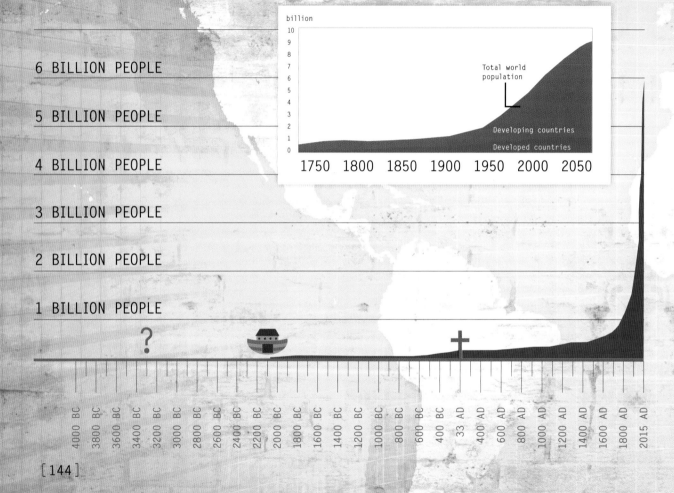

6 BILLION PEOPLE

5 BILLION PEOPLE

4 BILLION PEOPLE

3 BILLION PEOPLE

2 BILLION PEOPLE

1 BILLION PEOPLE

billion

10
9
8
7
6
5
4
3
2
1
0

Total world population

Developing countries

Developed countries

1750 1800 1850 1900 1950 2000 2050

?

4000 BC 3800 BC 3600 BC 3400 BC 3200 BC 3000 BC 2800 BC 2600 BC 2400 BC 2200 BC 2000 BC 1800 BC 1600 BC 1400 BC 1200 BC 1000 BC 800 BC 600 BC 400 BC 33 AD 400 AD 600 AD 800 AD 1000 AD 1200 AD 1400 AD 1600 AD 1800 AD 2015 AD

1975 2000

4 BILLION   6 BILLION

In 1975 there were 4 billion people living on the globe. This means that in just 25 years, 7 times as many people were added to the world's population than the total population while Jesus was here.

Between 1975 and 2000, world population jumped 50%, from 4 billion to 6 billion people. However, as we can see from the small inset chart,[42] this tremendous growth occurred almost entirely in poor or developing countries.

[145]

7 BILLION PEOPLE

6 BILLION PEOPLE

5 BILLION PEOPLE

4 BILLION PEOPLE

3 BILLION PEOPLE

2 BILLION PEOPLE

1 BILLION PEOPLE

4000 BC 3800 BC 3600 BC 3400 BC 3200 BC 3000 BC 2800 BC 2600 BC 2400 BC 2200 BC 2000 BC 1800 BC 1600 BC 1400 BC 1200 BC 1000 BC 800 BC 600 BC 400 BC 33 AD 400 AD 600 AD 800 AD 1000 AD 1200 AD 1400 AD 1600 AD 1800 AD 2015 AD

2012

7 BILLION

Then on March 12, 2012, the United States Census Bureau estimated that the world crossed the 7 billion mark. In just over 11 years, an additional 1 billion people had been added to the planet.

But there is something very important we need to note.

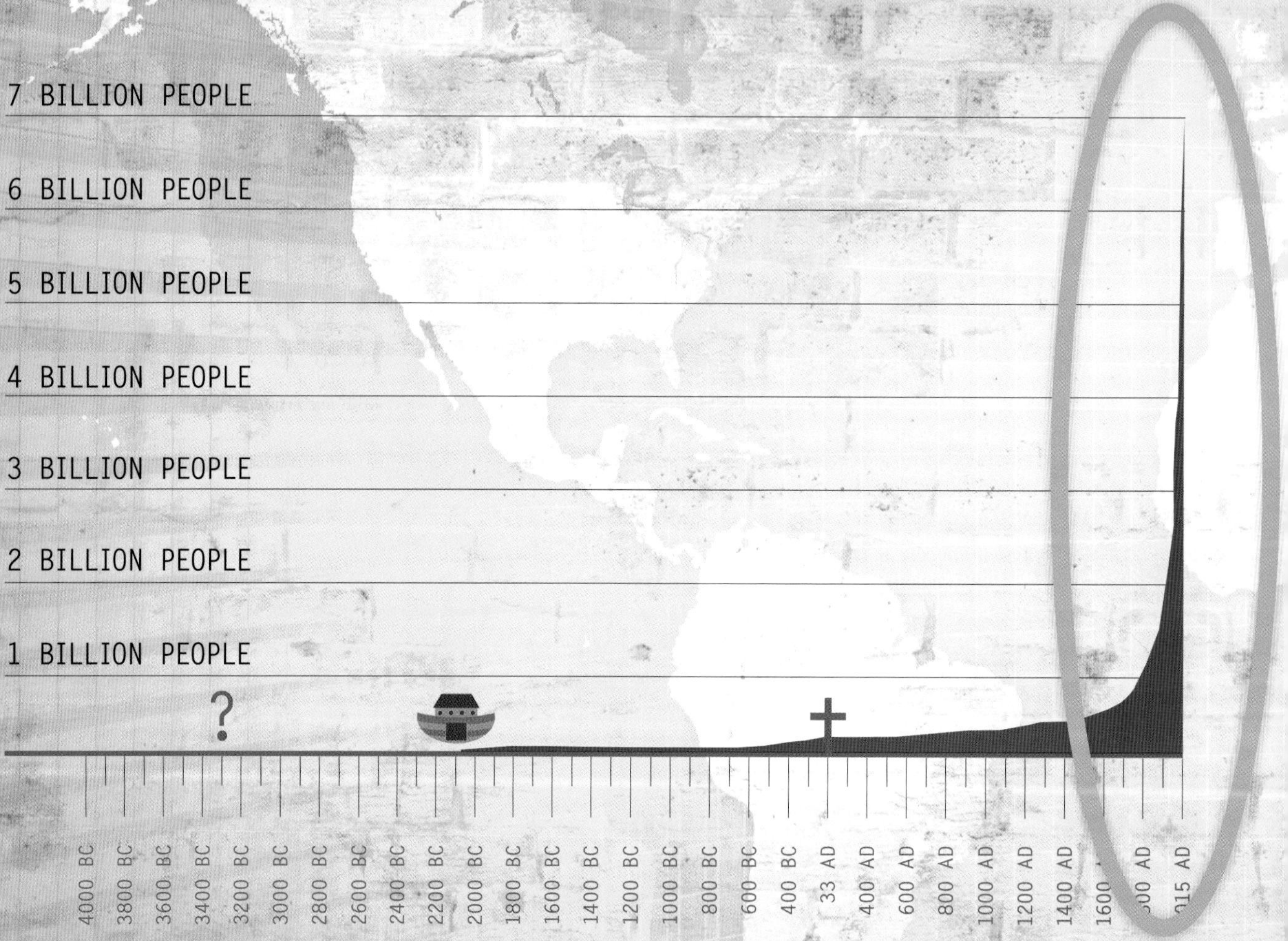

7 BILLION PEOPLE

6 BILLION PEOPLE

5 BILLION PEOPLE

4 BILLION PEOPLE

3 BILLION PEOPLE

2 BILLION PEOPLE

1 BILLION PEOPLE

4000 BC 3800 BC 3600 BC 3400 BC 3200 BC 3000 BC 2800 BC 2600 BC 2400 BC 2200 BC 2000 BC 1800 BC 1600 BC 1400 BC 1200 BC 1000 BC 800 BC 600 BC 400 BC 33 AD 400 AD 600 AD 800 AD 1000 AD 1200 AD 1400 AD 1600 AD 1800 AD 2015 AD

Notice the little window of time in which the majority of this great change took place. From a historical perspective, we live in an amazing time.

Way back between Noah's ark and the cross of Jesus, Moses told the children of Israel that they had become a mighty people. He said, "The Lord thy God hath made thee as the stars of heaven for multitude."[b] Yet when that was spoken, they barely show up on our timeline compared to world population today.

It is easy to see that astounding changes in population occurred in a very short period of time. But what might God be doing here at this time, and what should we be learning from this?

Let's look at another major change that has taken place.

---

[b] Deuteronomy 10:22

Communication

We have grown up with books, and it is hard to imagine life without them. But for many years there was no formalized way of writing. Stories were told about previous times, and knowledge was verbally passed on from generation to generation. Skilled storytellers held positions of honor in communities, and having a good memory was a tremendous blessing. This was all anyone knew, and it was normal for centuries.

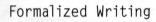
Formalized Writing

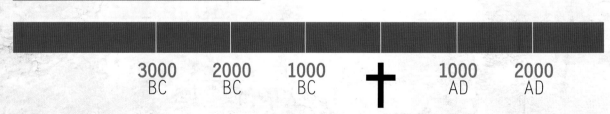

3000
BC

2000
BC

1000
BC

✝

1000
AD

2000
AD

We don't know exactly when, but sometime before Moses' time, men began to find ways to write their stories on rocks, dried animal skins, and eventually papyrus. For the first time, information could be stored and shared after a person died.

This must have seemed like an amazing invention to the people of that day. Yet because of the quality of ink and the nature of the material being written on, writings quickly decayed and information could soon be lost. So individuals constantly needed to copy old writings by hand to ensure that information was not lost. Due to the labor required, these writings were extremely valuable. We give little thought to this, but as each generation wrote down yet more information, copying remained an important occupation for thousands of years.

Printing Press

Formalized Writing

3000
BC

2000
BC

1000
BC

✝

1000
AD

2000
AD

Around 1450, new technology appeared. A man named Johannes Gutenberg invented a machine with movable type which could mechanically produce printed material much faster and more accurately than by hand. This was an incredible change!

Suddenly a man could mass-produce information and influence the thought pattern of entire nations without ever going to them! In our media-inundated world, it probably isn't possible for us to comprehend the significance of the printing press. Many have said it is the most important invention in the past thousand years. But looking back, we see this was only the beginning of the communication revolution.

Telegraph

Printing Press

Formalized Writing

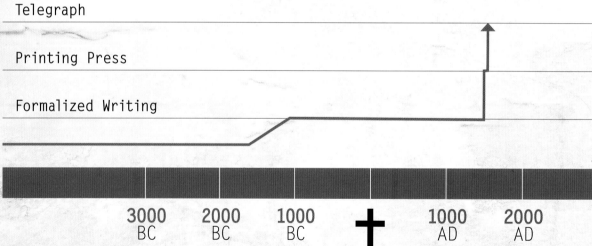

3000 BC   2000 BC   1000 BC   †   1000 AD   2000 AD

The development of the telegraph in the early 1800s transformed how men thought about communication. For the first time in human history, a message could be sent through a wire! Imagine—news events, military orders, or even personal messages could be sent from one city to another almost instantaneously! This amazing development must have seemed like magic.

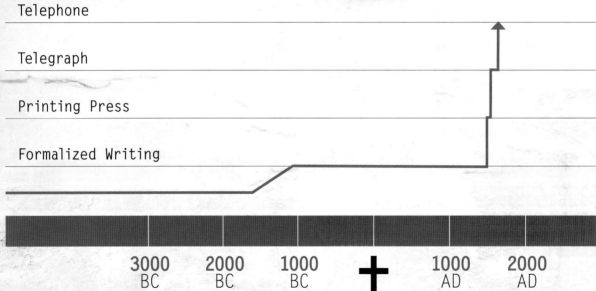

Telephone

Telegraph

Printing Press

Formalized Writing

| 3000 BC | 2000 BC | 1000 BC | ✝ | 1000 AD | 2000 AD |

Closely following the telegraph came the telephone. In 1876, Alexander Graham Bell applied for a patent for a machine that enabled a man to speak across a wire. Can you imagine the facial expressions of people who for the first time heard the familiar voice of a relative coming out of a box on the wall? In less than 50 years, communication had advanced from paper and ink to talking through a copper wire!

Radio

Telephone

Telegraph

Printing Press

Formalized Writing

3000 BC   2000 BC   1000 BC   ✝   1000 AD   2000 AD

The early 1900s brought an unprecedented rapid succession of marvelous inventions. First came the radio, with the first public broadcast in 1910. If people were astounded to hear voices through a copper wire, we can only imagine the incredulity of those first listening to news reports from hundreds of miles away that traveled on nothing but invisible air waves. Surely, people must have thought, communication couldn't advance any further than this.

From the first transatlantic telegraph cable laid in 1858 to the telephone cable inaugurated in 1956, many attempts were made to communicate across the Atlantic. Most of these attempts failed due to the many challenges and problems inherent to laying cables across thousands of miles of ocean floor.

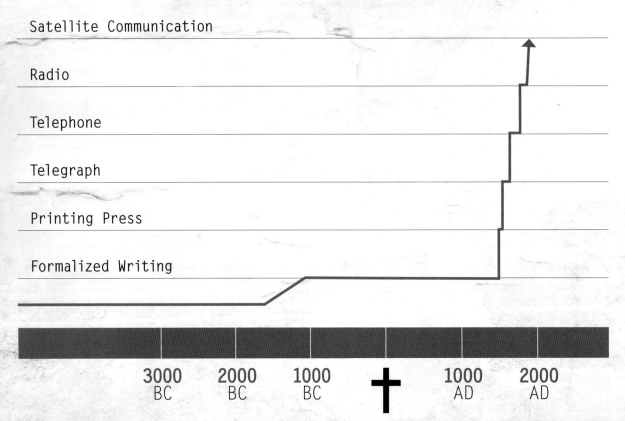

Satellite Communication

Radio

Telephone

Telegraph

Printing Press

Formalized Writing

3000
BC

2000
BC

1000
BC

✝

1000
AD

2000
AD

But in 1962 a huge communication milestone was reached that eliminated many of these obstacles.

A satellite, called the Telstar, was launched into space, enabling phone companies to transmit telephone conversations across the ocean without the use of wires. Satellites enabled men to instantly communicate with people on the other side of the world, regardless of their location or proximity to a landline.

What an amazing time to be alive, and again men must have thought they had reached the pinnacle of progress and communication!

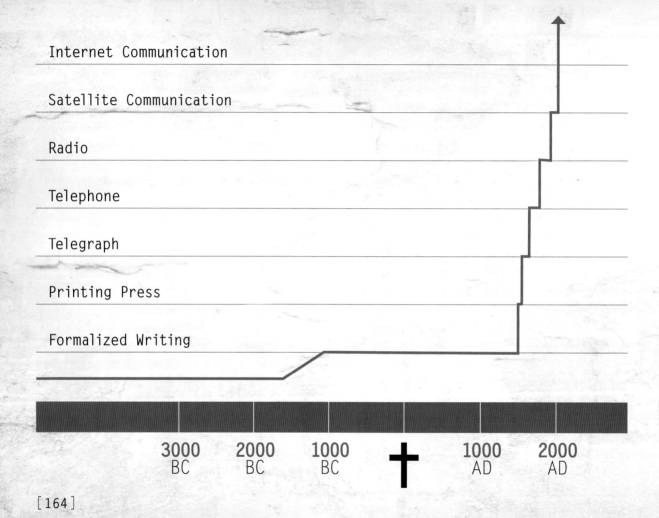

Internet Communication

Satellite Communication

Radio

Telephone

Telegraph

Printing Press

Formalized Writing

3000
BC

2000
BC

1000
BC

1000
AD

2000
AD

Today communication has advanced far beyond mere transmission of voice. Our airwaves are literally flooded with documents, financial transactions, pictures, as well as any other type of digital information one can upload to a computer. All of this is constantly being sent around the world at the speed of light.

Anyone in the farthest outreaches of Africa with access to an Internet connection can instantly know what is happening on Wall Street. Medical clinics in Sierra Leone can transmit X-rays or questions to doctors in a developed country with ease, and in the busyness of modern life, we have become accustomed to this incredible capability to communicate.

But there is something of great importance we should note.

All of this capability has been developed in just a little window of time. The world of communication has changed dramatically!

It is essential to understand that these changes are bringing unforeseen challenges. Young people today are thrust into a world of communication that has little resemblance to what their grandparents thought was normal. This has brought both tremendous challenge and opportunity. Ungodly information is flooding our world, leaving in its wake incredible spiritual damage.

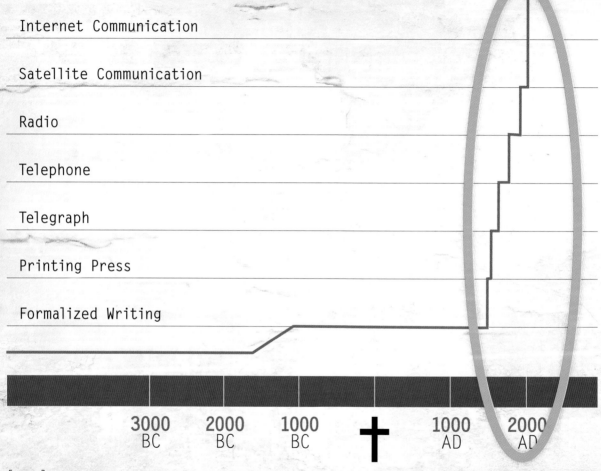

Internet Communication

Satellite Communication

Radio

Telephone

Telegraph

Printing Press

Formalized Writing

3000 BC   2000 BC   1000 BC   ✝   1000 AD   2000 AD

But there is also amazing potential for good. Today we can hear about more needs, assist in faraway places, and bless people in ways our ancestors couldn't have dreamed of. You can pick up a cell phone and encourage people in ways the Apostle Paul couldn't have imagined.

But look at the timeline again. Notice how much change has occurred in a very short time. What might God be trying to tell us today? Have we underestimated the import of the opportunity God has placed in our hands?

Let's look at another amazing global change.

Transportation

Distance Man Can Travel in One Day

For thousands of years, the farthest a man could travel in a day was around 40 miles. Caravans could travel 20 miles, ships up to 40 if the wind was right, and a man on horseback could travel as far as 40 miles in a day if he had a very good horse. Forty miles was a long distance, and the world must have seemed incredibly huge! When a man moved a few hundred miles away, others were well aware that they might not ever see him again.

200 Miles ——

100 Miles ——

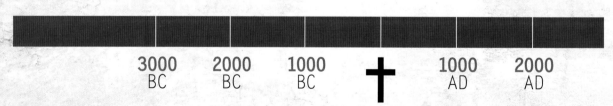

3000
BC

2000
BC

1000
BC

✝

1000
AD

2000
AD

Then in the early 1800s, the amazing development of the steam locomotive stunned the world. Several men began to grasp the potential of these "Iron Horses," and on September 15, 1830, one event upset thousands of years of history. English engineer George Stephenson was fueling his steam locomotive for its first trip when a man named William Huskisson was suddenly injured. George quickly disconnected the locomotive from the attached cars to rush after medical help for William. George's unburdened locomotive set a new speed record of 36 mph. In one hour his machine traveled almost as far as a man could travel in an entire day. What an achievement! Unfortunately, that speed was not enough to save William Huskisson's life. But men began to set their sights on achieving greater distances and speeds.[43]

Can you imagine what went through people's minds at that time? Thirty-six miles in one hour? That was an unheard of speed. How far could a man travel in a day if that speed could be sustained?

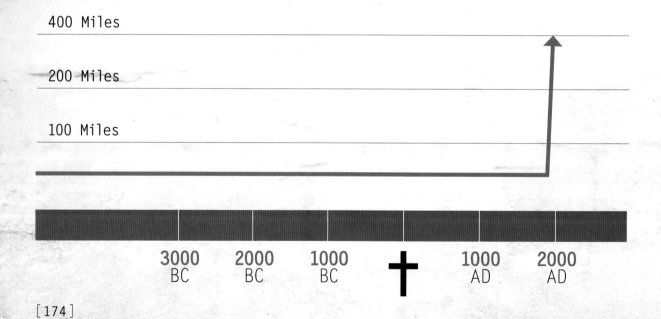

400 Miles

200 Miles

100 Miles

3000
BC

2000
BC

1000
BC

1000
AD

2000
AD

Following close on the heels of the steam engine came the internal combustion engine, and in 1908 Henry Ford introduced the famous Model T. This car had the ability to transport a family as fast as 45 mph, although few roads existed where this amazing speed could be reached. This meant that in one day people could travel up to 400 miles, 10 times the distance people for thousands of years could have hoped to travel in a day!

"I will build a car for the great multitude. It will be large enough for the family, but small enough for the individual to run and care for. It will be constructed of the best materials, by the best men to be hired, after the simplest designs that modern engineering can devise. But it will be so low in price that no man making a good salary will be unable to own one—and enjoy with his family the blessing of hours of pleasure in God's great open spaces."

—Henry Ford

3,200 Miles

1,600 Miles

800 Miles

400 Miles

200 Miles

100 Miles

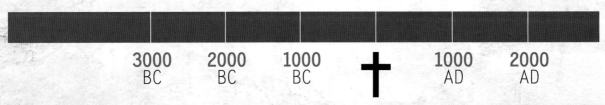

3000
BC

2000
BC

1000
BC

1000
AD

2000
AD

Then came the airplane, and on May 2, 1923, John A. Macready and Oakley G. Kelly flew a Fokker T-2 from Long Island, New York, to San Diego, California. This was the first nonstop transcontinental flight across the United States, traveling 2,520 miles in 27 hours. Again people marveled and wondered what could be next in this exciting new world of travel.

3,200 Miles

1,600 Miles

800 Miles

400 Miles

200 Miles

100 Miles

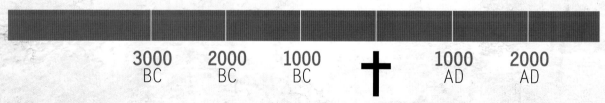

3000
BC

2000
BC

1000
BC

1000
AD

2000
AD

Of course, looking back we know that change in transportation continued to advance at an astounding pace. Many individuals born in the late 1800s, when horses were the primary mode of transportation, watched their televisions in amazement as Neil Armstrong stepped on the moon in 1969. In just 66 years, a time period so short it would barely show on our timeline, man went from the first flight at Kitty Hawk to a successful moon landing.

In fact, transportation changed so rapidly that the same people who migrated west by covered wagon in their youth, like Laura Ingalls Wilder, traveled by airplane in their older years.

Today, an individual can leave his home and be almost anywhere on the globe in just one day! What tremendous change!

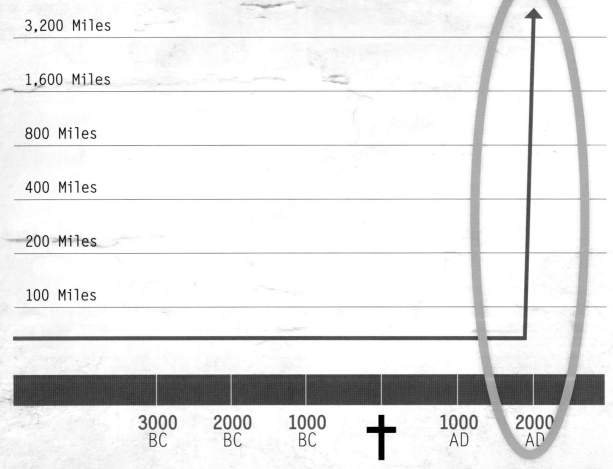

3,200 Miles

1,600 Miles

800 Miles

400 Miles

200 Miles

100 Miles

3000
BC

2000
BC

1000
BC

✝

1000
AD

2000
AD

But again, try to wrap your mind around the tiny space of time in which all this incredible change took place! In just a little sliver of the transportation timeline, man's thinking about the world, distance, and travel has been forever changed.

After Orville and Wilber Wright conquered the first challenge of getting their aircraft in the air, they faced the second challenge of putting it back on the ground with their bodies intact. But today, flying has become so common that many travelers, engrossed in a good book, don't even look out the window while landing.

What is happening to our world, and how should we regard these incredible changes? And more important, as God places all these resources and the accompanying opportunities into our hands, how should we be responding? We need to remember that not everyone on the globe has been affected by these changes in the same way.

In reality, this amazing ability to travel is only available to the relatively few who have the resources to make use of it.

THIS
SIDE OF
THE
GLOBAL WALL

We have looked at the great inequality in our world. A few have too much and many have too little. We have also looked at America, a country that is clearly sitting on the wealthy side of the global wall. And we must acknowledge that we live in an unparalleled time. Never in the history of man have so many opportunities been poured into the hands of so few.

So if you are alive today in a developed country like America, there is a question you need to ask yourself . . .

A Question You Need to

ANSWER

WHY AM I ON THIS SIDE OF THE WALL?

Of all the times, regimes, and economies in history when you could have been born, why did God place you right here, right now? In a world where over 3 billion people survive on less than $2.50 per day, why were you born in such an affluent setting?[44]

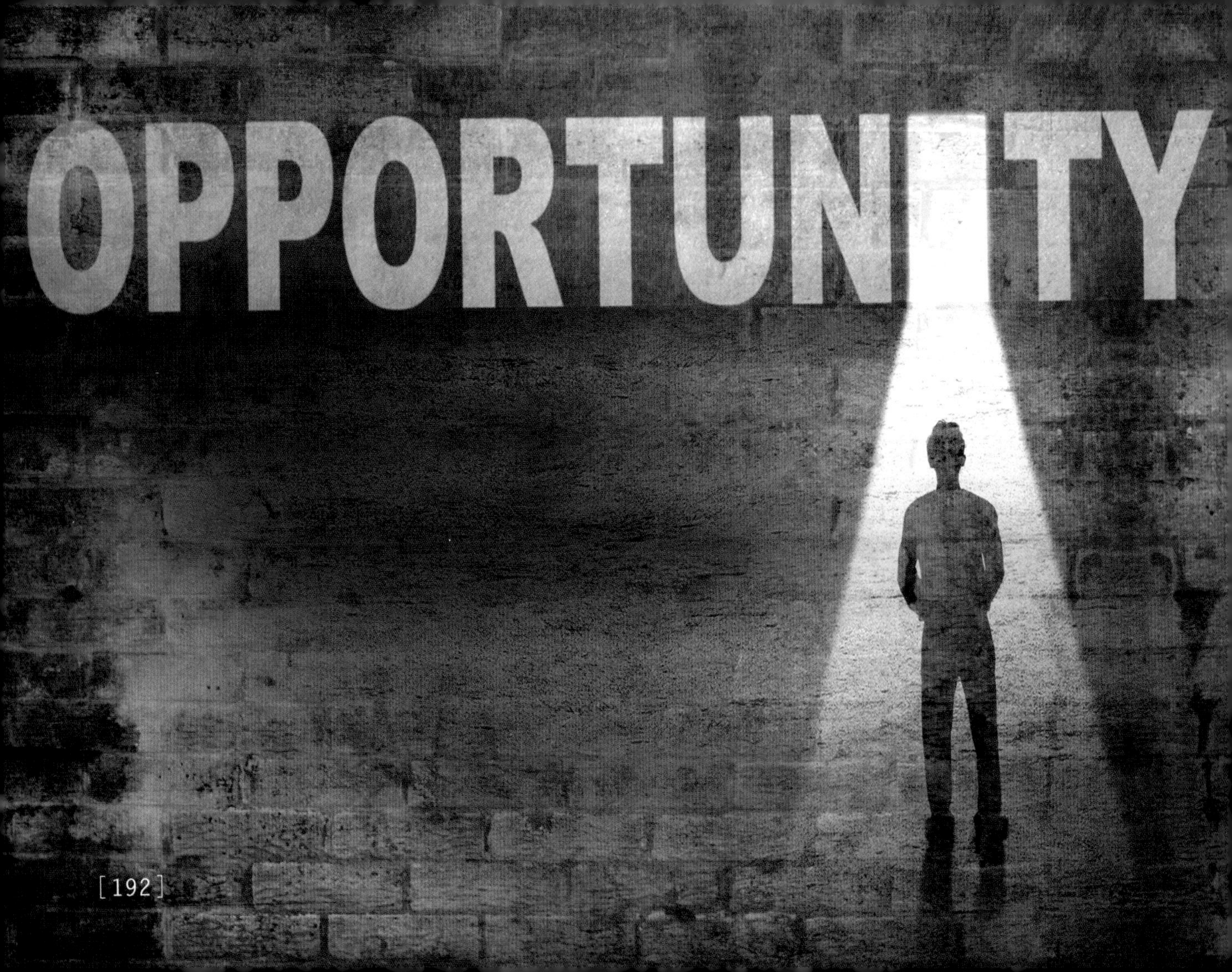
OPPORTUNITY

Why?

Anyone with even minimal reasoning capability is forced to ask some questions beginning with the word *why*. Why have so many resources been placed in the hands of so few? Why do many have difficulty finding food, while others spend billions on diet plans? Why are some geographical areas on the globe flourishing while others seem to languish? And from a historical perspective, why has so much change taken place in so short a period of time?

Today there are more opportunities to bless others, more people who have never heard the Gospel, and more ways to reach these people than ever before! In other words, there has never been a time in history when both the needs and the ways to meet those needs have been so abundant. And if you live on the wealthy side of the wall, there is a parable of Jesus you need to consider.

The Parable of the Talents

Jesus said that the Kingdom of heaven is like a wealthy man who entrusted his wealth to three stewards before he took a journey. To one he gave five talents of money, to another two, and to yet another just one. Upon returning from his trip, the wealthy man discovered that the servant who had received only one talent had buried it in the ground. This servant was afraid to take risk, intent on preserving what his lord had entrusted to him. But have you ever wondered why the wealthy owner was so angry at this?

The steward did return what had been given him. He could have stolen the talent or used it to purchase something for himself. Instead, he had kept the talent safe. Why didn't the lord at least commend this servant for faithful preservation? Instead, the returning lord angrily lashed out with, "Thou wicked and slothful servant . . ."[c]

Why such anger at this man? Because the lord, representing God in this parable, had expected his servants to put these talents to use. He wanted return on his investment, even if it involved risk in the marketplace! Jesus challenges and warns us in this parable that our God also desires increase. He gives resources to us, intending that we use them to further His Kingdom.

But have you ever wondered how the lord might have responded if the servant with five talents had buried them? If the lord was angry at a servant who had buried just one talent, what kind of wrath might he have had if a servant had buried five?

---

[c] Matthew 25:26

A Five-Talent Time

If you live on the wealthy side of the global wall, you are living in a five-talent time. So how are you using the resources God has given you? Do you have a vision for using them to further God's Kingdom? Do you, like God, have a vision for increase and growth? Or is it possible that you, like the unfaithful servant, have instead focused only on preserving what God has given you?

The potential sitting on the pews of conservative churches here in America is amazing. With our economic wealth, our heritage of strong communities, the blessing of living free of persecution, and our place on the historical timeline, our situation is truly unprecedented. We are living in a five-talent time! Yet with this great opportunity comes something else.

A Time of Great Distraction

Our culture of plenty provides an almost infinite array of diversions, and we tend to forget why God has given us so much. Like the lepers outside Samaria,[d] we get caught up in enjoying the plenty and forget the great need on the other side of the wall. We forget global disparity and the great Kingdom opportunities we're missing.

But there is something else we forget. We forget that this wonderful opportunity will soon be gone. The Apostle Peter said it like this: "Seeing then that all these things shall be dissolved, what manner of persons ought ye to be in all holy conversation and godliness?"[e] In

---

[d] 2 Kings 7

[e] 2 Peter 3:11

other words, since everything around us will soon be gone, shouldn't our lives be focused on the Kingdom? Shouldn't all our tangible and intangible resources be flowing toward eternal things?

Conclusion

These questions could mean different things to different people. Maybe God is calling you to stop burying your resources and invest them in His Kingdom instead. Perhaps you are caught up in the materialistic distractions that Satan daily dangles before you. Or maybe you have been a sleepy steward who just needs to be stirred to action.

Whatever your situation, purpose to pour your resources, your energy, and your passion into the Kingdom of God. Maybe God is calling you to go across the ocean to bless others. But it is also possible He is calling you to simply go across the street to reach out to a neighbor. Whatever your calling, understand that you live in a world of opportunity, and God expects a return on His investment in your life. Purpose to use all He has given you for His glory and Kingdom!

Endnotes

Note: I have tried to find as accurate numbers as possible for each statistic. In some cases, this meant averaging statistics from various sources. The numbers in this book are approximate, intended to give an overall picture of our world, and they are always changing. —Gary Miller

[1] Gary Miller, *The Other Side of the Wall,* TGS International, Berlin, OH, 2013, pp. 1–2.

[2] Richard Kersley, Michael O'Sullivan, and Cushla Sherlock, "Global Wealth Reaches New All-Time High," *Credit Suisse,* September 10, 2013, <https://www.credit-suisse.com/us/en/news-and-expertise/research/credit-suisse-research-institute/news-and-videos.article.html/article/pwp/news-and-expertise/2013/10/en/global-wealth-reaches-new-all-time-high.html>, accessed on May 4, 2015.

[3] "Working for the Few," *Oxfam,* January 20, 2014, <http://www.oxfam.org/sites/www.oxfam.org/files/file_attach-ments/bp-working-for-few-political-capture-economic-inequality-200114-en_3.pdf>, accessed on May 4, 2015.

[4] Sean Levinson, "This Map Shows How Individual States' GDPs Compare To Countries Around The World," *Elite Daily,* February 4, 2014, <http://elitedaily.com/news/business/map-shows-individual-states-gdps-compare-countries-around-world-photo/>, accessed on May 4, 2015.

CIA World Factbook, <https://www.cia.gov/library/publi-cations/the-world-factbook/>, accessed on May 4, 2015.

[5] Jens Manuel Krogstad and Mark Hugo Lopez, "Hispanic Nativity Shift," *Pew Research Center,* April 29, 2014, <www.

pewhispanic.org/2014/04/29/hispanic-nativity-shift/>, accessed on May 4, 2015.

6 <http://www.merriam-webster.com/dictionary/african-american>, accessed on May 4, 2015.

7 "America's Foreign Born in the Last 50 Years," *United States Census Bureau,* February 13, 2013, <https://www.census.gov/library/infographics/foreign_born.html>, accessed on May 4, 2015.

8 Nate Berg, "U.S. Urban Population Is Up ... But What Does 'Urban' Really Mean?" Citylab, March 26, 2012, <http://www.citylab.com/housing/2012/03/us-urban-population-what/1589/>, accessed on May 4, 2015.

9 <http://quickfacts.census.gov/qfd/states/00000.html>, accessed on May 5, 2015.

Cindy Kent, "21 million Americans have paid-off Mortgages," *Sun Sentinel,* January 11, 2013, <http://articles.sun-sentinel.com/2013-01-11/business/fl-home-free-tophat-20130111_1_mortgages-zillow-homeowners>, accessed on May 5, 2015.

10 "Homelessness / Poverty Statistics," *Statistic Brain Research Institute,* April 20, 2015, <http://www.statisticbrain.com/homelessness-stats/>, accessed on May 5, 2015.

11 "Religious Landscape Study," *Pew Research Center,* <http://www.pewforum.org/religious-landscape-study/>, accessed on May 5, 2015.

Cathy Lynn Grossman, "As Protestants decline, those with no religion gain," USA Today, October 9, 2012, <http://www.usatoday.com/story/news/nation/2012/10/08/nones-protestant-religion-pew/1618445/>, accessed on May 5, 2015.

12 Young Center for Anabaptist and Pietist Studies, Elizabethtown College, 1 Alpha Drive, Elizabethtown, PA, 17022.

13 Young Center for Anabaptist and Pietist Studies, Elizabethtown College, 1 Alpha Drive, Elizabethtown, PA, 17022.

"Hutterian Brethren," <http://www.hutterites.org/the-leut/distribution/>, accessed on May 7, 2015.

14 Kelly Shattuck, "7 Startling Facts: An Up Close Look at Church Attendance in America," *Church Leaders,* <http://www.churchleaders.com/pastors/pastor-articles/139575-7-startling-facts-an-up-close-look-at-church-attendance-in-america.html>, accessed on May 7, 2015.

15 Jasmin, "Divorce in America," *Daily Infographic,* October 24, 2013, <http://dailyinfographic.com/divorce-in-america-infographic>, accessed on May 7, 2015.

16 Luke Rosiak, "Fathers disappear from households

across America," *The Washington Times,* December 25, 2012, <http://www.washingtontimes.com/news/2012/dec/25/fathers-disappear-from-households-across-america/#ixzz3CreSN2vY>, accessed on May 7, 2015.

[17] *Prison Policy Initiative,* 2014, <http://www.prisonpolicy.org/graphs/US_federal_incrates_1978-2012.html>, accessed on May 7, 2015.

[18] Bob Linton, "70% Of Criminals Are From Broken Homes, Expert Says," *The Morning Call,* November 15, 1991, <http://www.articles.mcall.com/1991-11-15/news/2826825_1_inmates-psychology-professor-raymond-bell>, accessed on May 7, 2015.

[19] Derek Thompson, "Cheap Eats: How America Spends Money on Food," *The Atlantic,* March 8, 2013, <http://www.theatlantic.com/business/archive/2013/03/cheap-eats-how-america-spends-money-on-food/273811/consuming_more_calories>, accessed on May 7, 2015.

[20] *ChartsBin,* 2011, <http://chartsbin.com/view/1150>, accessed on May 9, 2015.

National Geographic, 2011, <http://www.nationalgeographic.com/what-the-world-eats/>, accessed on May 9, 2015.

[21] <http://www.infoplease.com/askeds/promising-chicken-every-pot.html>, accessed on May 9, 2015.

<http://www.presidentsusa.net/1928slogan.html>, accessed on May 9, 2015.

[22] *American Journal of Preventive Medicine.*

[23] Associated Press, "Feds: Obesity raising airline fuel costs," *USA Today,* November 7, 2004, <http://usatoday30.usatoday.com/travel/news/2004-11-05-obese-fliers_x.htm>, accessed on May 9, 2015.

"Southwest will charge large fliers extra fare," *The Washington Times,* June 19, 2002, <http://www.washingtontimes.com/news/2002/jun/19/20020619-032011-2887r/?page=all>, accessed on May 11, 2015.

[24] Carl Campanile, "Americans are getting fatter: poll," *New York Post,* November 23, 2012, <http://nypost.com/2012/11/23/americans-are-getting-fatter-poll>, accessed on May 11, 2015.

[25] *National Institute of Diabetes and Digestive and Kidney Diseases,* 2010, <http://www.niddk.nih.gov/health-information/health-statistics/Pages/overweight-obesity-statistics.aspx>, accessed on May 11, 2015.

Dr. Leo Galland, M.D., "Solving America's Obesity Crisis,"

The Christian Broadcasting Network, 2010, <http://www.cbn.com/health/weightloss/fatresistance_galland.aspx>, accessed on May 11, 2015.

[26] Nanci Hellmich, "Percentage of severely obese adults skyrockets," *USA Today,* October 1, 2012, <http://www.usatoday.com/story/news/nation/2012/10/01/severely-obese-americans-increasing/1606469/>, accessed on May 11, 2015.

[27] Rachel Pomerance Berl, "Why We're So Fat: What's Behind the Latest Obesity Rates," *U.S. News,* August 16, 2012, <http://health.usnews.com/health-news/articles/2012/08/16/why-were-so-fat-whats-behind-the-latest-obesity-rates>, accessed on May 11, 2015.

[28] Eliza Barclay, "Your Grandparents Spent More Of Their Money On Food Than You Do," *NPR The Salt,* March 2, 2015, <http://www.npr.org/sections/the-salt/2015/03/02/389578089/your-grandparents-spent-more-of-their-money-on-food-than-you-do>, accessed on May 11, 2015.

Derek Thompson, "How America Spends Money: 100 Years in the Life of the Family Budget," *The Atlantic,* April 5, 2012, <http://www.theatlantic.com/business/archive/2012/04/how-america-spends-money-100-years-in-the-life-of-the-family-budget/255475>, accessed on May 11, 2015.

[29] *USDA,* 2014-2015, <http://www.ers.usda.gov/data-products/food-expenditures.aspx#.U2qL1vldXTo>, accessed on May 11, 2015.

[30] The Economist, "Thought for food," March 12, 2013, <http://www.economist.com/blogs/graphicdetail/2013/03/daily-chart-5>, accessed on May 13, 2015.

[31] The Associated Press, "Americans spent a record $56 billion on pets last year," *CBS News,* March 13, 2014, <http://www.cbsnews.com/news/americans-spent-a-record-56-billion-on-pets-last-year/>, accessed on May 13, 2015.

[32] Lucas Reilley, "By the Numbers: How Americans Spend Their Money," *Mental Floss,* July 7, 2012, <http://www.mentalfloss.com/article/31222/numbers-how-americans-spend-their-money>, accessed on May 13, 2015.

[33] "America Spends More Money on Lawn Care than Foreign Aid: Why We Need Less Lawn," *People Powered Machines,* December 16, 2008, <https://peoplepoweredmachines.wordpress.com/2008/12/16/america-spends-more-money-on-lawn-care-than-foreign-aid-why-we-need-less-lawn/>, accessed on May 13, 2015.

34 "Car Wash Industry Statistics," *Statistic Brain Research Institute,* February 2, 2015, <http://www.statisticbrain.com/car-wash-car-detail-industry-stats/>, accessed on May 15, 2015.

35 "2011 National Survey of Fishing, Hunting, and Wildlife-Associated Recreation," *U.S. Fish & Wildlife Service,* <https://www.census.gov/prod/2012pubs/fhw11-nat.pdf>, accessed on May 15, 2015.

"Hunting Statistics," *Statistic Brain Research Institute,* March 20, 2012, <http://www.statisticbrain.com/hunting-statistics/>, accessed on May 15, 2015.

"Statistics and facts on recreational fishing," *Statista,* 2014, <http://www.statista.com/topics/1163/recreational-fishing/>, accessed on May 15, 2015.

36 "Price of Safe Water for All: $10 Billion and the Will to Provide It," *The New York Times,* November 23, 2000, <http://www.nytimes.com/2000/11/23/world/price-of-safe-water-for-all-10-billion-and-the-will-to-provide-it.html>, accessed on May 18, 2015.

37 Fahad Al-Sulaiti, "Counting the cost of universal primary Education," *The Guardian,* November 28, 2013, <http://www.theguardian.com/global-development-professionals-network/2013/nov/28/universal-primary-education-cost-fund>, accessed on May 18, 2015.

38 "Charitable Giving Statistics," *National Philanthropic Trust,* 2015, <http://www.nptrust.org/philanthropic-resources/charitable-giving-statistics/>, accessed on May 20, 2015.

39 "Giving USA: Americans Gave $335.17 Billion to Charity in 2013; Total Approaches Pre-Recession Peak," Indiana *University Lilly Family School of Philanthropy,* June 17, 2014, <http://www.philanthropy.iupui.edu/news/article/giving-usa-2014>, accessed on May 20, 2015.

40 "Myths About Aid," *Giving What We Can,* 2013, <http://www.givingwhatwecan.org/get-involved/myths-about-aid>, accessed on May 20, 2015.

41 "World Population," *United States Census Bureau,* 2014, <https://www.census.gov/population/international/data/worldpop/table_history.php>, accessed on May 21, 2015.

42 "World Population Growth," <http://www.worldbank.org/depweb/english/beyond/beyondco/beg_03.pdf>, accessed May 21, 2015.

43 *Ward's Book of Days,* 2006, <http://www.wardsbookof-days.com/15september.htm>, accessed on August 13, 2015.

44 Anup Shah, "Poverty Facts and Stats," *Global Issues,* January 7, 2013, <http://www.globalissues.org/article/26/poverty-facts-and-stats>, accessed on May 21, 2015.

Other Resources by the Author

Gary Miller was raised in an Anabaptist community in California and today lives with his wife Patty and family in the Pacific Northwest. Gary's enthusiasm for Kingdom building has prompted him to produce the resources listed on this page and the next, all published by TGS International.

KINGDOM-FOCUSED LIVING SERIES

Kingdom-Focused Finances for the Family | This first book is serious about getting us to become stewards instead of owners. *240 pages*

Charting a Course in Your Youth | A serious call to youth to examine their faith, focus, and finances. *211 pages*

Going Till You're Gone | A plea for older men and women to demonstrate a Kingdom-focused vision all the way to the finish line. *281 pages*

The Other Side of the Wall | Encourages all Christians to reflect God's heart in giving, whether by helping in their local community or by seeking to alleviate poverty abroad. *250 pages*

It's Not Your Business | Could God have a deeper purpose for our businesses than we have realized? What if occupational life, from God's perspective, is intended to play a prominent role in His Kingdom? *260 pages*

OTHER BOOKS/MANUALS

Budgeting Made Simple | A budgeting workbook in a ring binder; complements *Kingdom-Focused Finances for the Family.*

What Happened to Our Money? | An introductory financial guide for young couples. *4.25" x 7"* | *86 pages*

Life in a Global Village | Would your perspective and lifestyle change if the world's population were shrunk to a village of 100 people, and you lived in that village? *6" x 8"* | *112 pages*

Small Business Handbook | A microfinance manual used in developing countries. Includes devotionals and practical business teaching. Ideal for missions and churches. *8.5" x 11"* | *spiral bound* | *136 pages*

Following Jesus in Everyday Life | A second microfinance manual that sets the stage for group discussions on how to follow Jesus daily in personal and business matters. *8.5" x 11"* | *spiral bound* | *93 pages*

A Good Soldier of Jesus Christ | A teaching manual like *Following Jesus in Everyday Life*, but targeting youth. *8.5" x 11"* | *spiral bound* | *93 pages*

AUDIO AND POWER POINT SEMINARS

Kingdom-Focused Finances Seminar—3 audio CDs
This three-session seminar challenges you to examine your heart by looking at your treasure.

Kingdom-Focused Finances Seminar Audio PowerPoint—3 CDs
On your computer, you can now view the slides Gary uses in his seminars while you listen to the presentation. A good tool for group study or individual use.

AUDIO BOOKS

Kingdom-Focused Finances for the Family, Charting a Course in Your Youth, Going Till You're Gone, The Other Side of the Wall, and **Life in a Global Village.**